Twenty First Century

SCI●NCE

REVISION

GCSE

Physics

Philippa Gardom Hulme
and
Hillary Taunton

OXFORD

UNIVERSITY PRESS

OXFORD
UNIVERSITY PRESS

Great Clarendon Street, Oxford OX2 6DP

Oxford University Press is a department of the University of Oxford.
It furthers the University's objective of excellence in research, scholarship,
and education by publishing worldwide in

Oxford   New York

Auckland   Cape Town   Dar es Salaam   Hong Kong   Karachi
Kuala Lumpur   Madrid   Melbourne   Mexico City   Nairobi
New Delhi   Shanghai   Taipei   Toronto

With offices in

Argentina   Austria   Brazil   Chile   Czech Republic   France   Greece
Guatemala   Hungary   Italy   Japan   Poland   Portugal   Singapore
South Korea   Switzerland   Thailand   Turkey   Ukraine   Vietnam

© University of York on behalf of UYSEG and the Nuffield Foundation 2006

British Library Cataloguing in Publication Data

Data available

ISBN: 978 019915 238 4

10 9 8 7 6 5

Printed in Great Britain Bell and Bain Ltd Glasgow

Author Acknowledgements
Thanks to Barney for all the ideas and constructive criticism. Thanks to Mum for some of the puzzles, and Mum
and Dad for help with checking. Thanks to Catherine and Sarah for keeping out of the study – and to Barney,
Mum, Dad and Helen for keeping them happy!

Philippa Gardom Hulme P1–P6

To Ruth, in the hope that this may be of some use to you! And with thanks to Dad for trying out all the questions
before publication.

Hillary Taunton, P7

Many people from schools, colleges, universities, industry, and the professions have contributed to the
production of these resources. The feedback from over 75 Pilot Centres was invaluable. It led to significant
changes to the course specifications, and to the supporting resources for teaching and learning.

The University of York Science Education Group (UYSEG) and Nuffield Curriculum Centre worked in partnership
with an OCR team led by Mary Whitehouse, Elizabeth Herbert and Emily Clare to create the specifications,
which have their origins in the Beyond 2000 report (Millar & Osborne, 1998) and subsequent Key Stage 4
development work undertaken by UYSEG and the Nuffield Curriculum Centre for QCA. Bryan Milner and Michael
Reiss also contributed to this work, which is reported in: 21st Century Science GCSE Pilot Development: Final
Report (UYSEG, March 2002).

Sponsors
The development of Twenty First Century Science was made possible by generous support from:
• The Nuffield Foundation
• The Salters' Institute
• The Wellcome Trust

THE SALTERS' INSTITUTE

Mixed Sources
Product group from well-managed
forests and other controlled sources
www.fsc.org   Cert no. TT-COC-002769
© 1996 Forest Stewardship Council

Contents

---

*The OCR specification describes six Ideas about Science. (Details of these are in Appendix F of the specification.):
  1 Data and their limitations
  2 Correlation and cause
  3 Developing explanations
  4 The scientific community
  5 Risk
  6 Making decisions about science and technology

Two different Ideas about Science are included in each of our Revision Guides: GCSE Biology, GCSE Chemistry, and GCSE Physics. You need to learn about all six Ideas. The OCR specifications show which Ideas about Science are associated with each module. The Unit 1 written paper, covering modules 1 to 3, assesses these Ideas about Science. You may be expected to use additional Ideas about Science in your coursework and the Unit 3 Ideas in Context paper.

If you are not using each of the GCSE Biology, GCSE Chemistry, and GCSE Physics Revision Guides, then you will need to other resources to revise all six Ideas about Science.

About this book

To parents and carers

This book is designed to help students achieve their best in OCR's Twenty First Century GCSE Physics examination. It includes sections on each of the areas of physics explored by Twenty First Century Science.

This book is designed to be used! Students will get the most from it if they do as many of the Workout and GCSE-style questions as possible. Many students will also find it helpful to highlight, colour, and scribble extra notes in the Fact banks.

To students

This book is in ten sections. There is one section for each physics modules P1 to P6, and four sections (A to D) for module P7.

Each section includes:

Workout

Go through these on your own or with a friend. Write your answers in the book. If you get stuck, look in the Fact bank. The index will help you to find what you need. Check your answers at the back of the book.

Fact bank

Each fact bank summarizes information from the module in just six pages. Don't just read the Fact banks – highlight key points, scribble extra details in the margin or on sticky notes, and make up ways to help you remember things. The messier this book is by the time you take your exams, the better!

You could try getting a friend – or someone at home – to test you on the Fact banks. Or make cards to test yourself. These could have

❯ a question on one side and an answer on the other or
❯ a word on one side and its definition on the other

GCSE-style questions

These are very like the module test questions. All the answers are at the back of the book.

In every section, content required for Higher level only is shown like this: **H**

Skills assessment: case study, data analysis, and investigation

Turn to pages 161–166 for a summary of essential advice on maximizing your marks in these assessment tasks.

1

D

C

B

A

This diagram shows sedimentary rock containing fossils. Assume that this rock has never been folded.

Give the letter of

a the layer that contains the youngest fossils _____

b the layer made of the oldest rocks _____

c the layer made of the youngest rocks _____

d the layer in which sediments were first deposited _____

2 Write the correct numbers in the gaps. Use the numbers in the box.

3 hundred thousand	**10**	**4 thousand million**
1000	**1.4 million**	**12 700**

a Light travels at _____ km/s.

b The Earth's oldest rocks are _____ years old.

c Seafloors spread by about _____ cm each year.

d The diameter of the Earth is _____ km.

e The diameter of the Sun is about _____ km.

f The diameter of the biggest asteroid in our Solar System is _____ km.

3 Draw a (ring) round the correct **bold** words.

Distant galaxies are moving **towards / away** from us.

H The graph shows that as the distance of a galaxy from the Milky Way increases, the speed at which the galaxy moves away from us **increases / decreases.** This is **Hubble's / Hutton's / Hawking's** law.

These galaxy movements mean that space is **getting smaller / expanding,** and also provide evidence that the Universe began with a 'big bang' fourteen **hundred / thousand / million** million years ago.

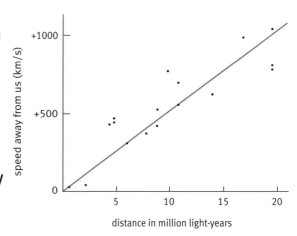

5

4 This question is about the possible ultimate fate of the Universe.

Label the graph below by writing one letter on each line.

A The Universe will reach a maximum size and then stop.

B The Universe will collapse with a 'big crunch'.

C The Universe will expand forever.

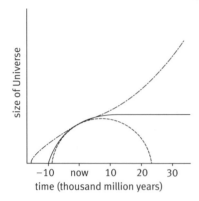

5 Finish the notes about volcanoes and earthquakes.

▶ A **volcano** is _____

Volcanoes are usually found at _____

Signs that a volcano will erupt soon are _____

_____

Authorities can reduce the damage caused by a volcano by _____

_____

_____

▶ An **earthquake** is _____

Earthquakes usually happen at _____

These types of movement cause earthquakes: _____

_____

_____

Authorities can reduce the damage caused by earthquakes by _____

_____

_____

What do we know about the Earth's structure, and how it changes?

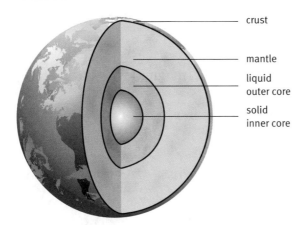

- crust
- mantle
- liquid outer core
- solid inner core

Evidence from rocks tells us about the structure of the Earth. For example, the Earth must be older than its oldest rocks. Scientists use **radioactive dating** to estimate rocks' ages.

Rock processes we see today explain past changes. For example, mountains are being made all the time – if not, **erosion** would wear down the continents to sea level.

Wegener's theory of continental drift (1912)

Wegener's theory states that today's continents were once joined together as one huge continent. They have been slowly moving for millions of years.

See page 134 for more details about Wegener's theory.

250 million years ago

Theory of seafloor spreading (1960s)

Geologists detected **oceanic ridges**, which are lines of mountains under the sea. They noticed a symmetrical stripe pattern in rock magnetism on each side of these ridges. They devised this explanation:

> New ocean floor is made at oceanic ridges, so oceans spread by about 10 cm a year.

The new ocean floor is made like this:

> Hot mantle rises beneath the ridge. It melts to make magma. Magma erupts at the middle of the ridge. It cools to make new rock. The new rock is magnetized in the direction of the Earth's field at the time.

The theory of plate tectonics (1967 onwards)

The outer layer of the Earth is made of about 12 huge pieces of rock, called **tectonic plates**. They move slowly all the time. Earthquakes, volcanoes, and mountain building usually happen where tectonic plates meet.

- **Plates move apart** at oceanic ridges. Molten rock (magma) rises up between the plates.
- In the Himalayas, **plates move towards each other**. They collide. Huge pressure makes rocks fold over on top of each other to **build mountains**.
- Most **volcanoes** are at plate boundaries where the crust is stretching or being compressed. Magma erupts out of a hole in the Earth's surface. Geologists monitor volcanoes carefully. They look for changes in the gases emitted and the swelling of a volcano's sides. If a volcano is likely to erupt the government may evacuate the area.
- Most **earthquakes** happen at rock breaks, called faults. The blocks of rock on each side of the fault move. Pressure builds up until the rocks snap.

In some places at risk from earthquakes, buildings must be built to withstand earthquake damage. Scientists cannot predict when earthquakes will strike.

- The movement of tectonic plates contributes to the **rock cycle**.

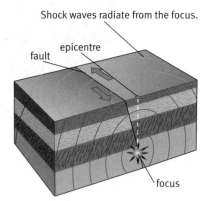

Shock waves radiate from the focus.
epicentre
fault
focus

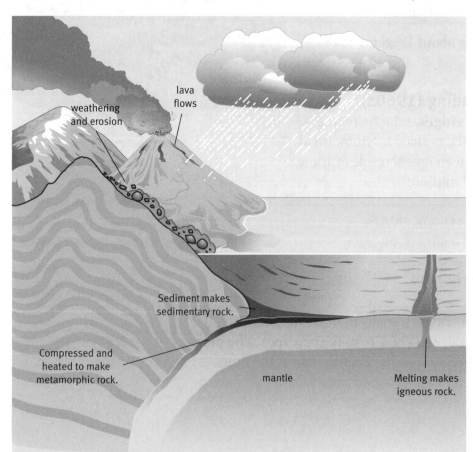

weathering and erosion

lava flows

Sediment makes sedimentary rock.

Compressed and heated to make metamorphic rock.

mantle

Melting makes igneous rock.

What do we know about our Solar System?

Our **Solar System** was formed from clouds of gases and dust in space.

The **Sun** is a star at the centre of the Solar System. It will probably shine for another 5000 million years. A **star** is a ball of hot gases, mainly hydrogen. In stars like the Sun, hydrogen nuclei join together (fuse) to make helium nuclei. This is the source of stars' energy. Stars change over time – they have a **life cycle**.

Eight **planets**, including Earth, orbit the Sun. Pluto used to be regarded as the ninth planet in our Solar System, but in August 2006 the scientists of the International Astronomical Union voted to reclassify Pluto as a 'dwarf planet'. Some planets have natural satellites (**moons**) that orbit them. **Comets** are lumps of rock held together by ice and frozen gases.

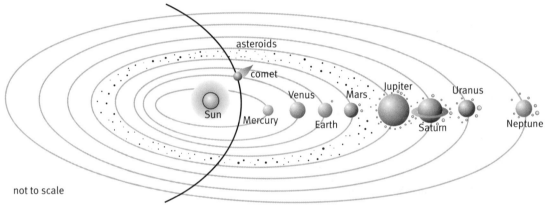

not to scale

Asteroids are lumps of rock that are much smaller than planets. Most asteroids orbit the Sun between Mars and Jupiter, but a few cross the Earth's path. There is a tiny risk that one of these asteroids will collide with Earth. If this happens, many people will die. An asteroid collision may have led to the extinction of dinosaurs 65 million years ago.

Type of body	Diameter	Age
planet	Mercury = 4880 km (smallest) Saturn = 120 000 km (biggest) Earth = 12 700 km	The Solar System was formed about 5000 million years ago.
moon	Earth's Moon = 3500 km Moons are smaller than the planets they orbit.	The Earth is older than its oldest rocks, which are 4000 million years old.
asteroid	up to 1000 km; most are much smaller.	
comet	a few km	
Sun	1.4 million km	5000 million years
Universe	many millions of times greater than the diameter of the Solar System	14 000 million years

What do we know about stars, galaxies, and the Universe?

Our Solar System is part of the Milky Way galaxy. **Galaxies** contain thousands of millions of stars. The **Universe** is made of thousands of millions of galaxies.

Other galaxies are moving away from us, because space is expanding. Hubble discovered that galaxies that are further away from us move faster than those that are closer to us. This is evidence that the Universe started with a '**big bang**'.

We do not know what will happen to the Universe; scientists disagree about how to interpret evidence about its final fate. Maybe the Universe will continue to expand. Or perhaps the force of gravity will attract galaxies towards each other again and the Universe will end with a 'big crunch'.

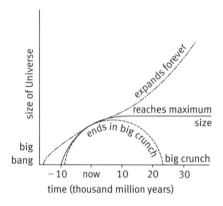

Is there life elsewhere in the Universe?

Scientists have detected planets around some stars. Life may exist on other planets in the Universe, but there is so far no evidence for this.

How do scientists find out about distant stars and galaxies?

Scientists can learn about other stars and galaxies only by studying the radiation they emit. They measure the distance to stars by looking at their relative **brightness** or by **parallax**. It is difficult to make accurate observations, so scientists do not know exact distances between objects in space.

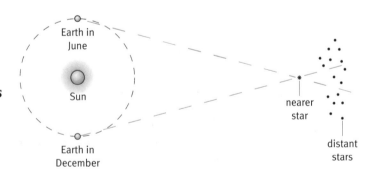

Light travels at 300 000 km/s. So when scientists observe distant objects they see what the object looked like when the light left the object – not what it looks like now. Scientists measure distances in space in light-years. One light-year is the distance light travels in one year.

Light pollution near cities makes it difficult to see stars, so scientists set up telescopes in areas of darkness away from cities.

The Earth moves from one side of the Sun to the other. Nearby stars seem to move compared to the background of distant stars. The nearer a star is to Earth, the more it seems to move. This is **parallax**.

1 a Write the following in order of age:

Earth   **Sun**   **Universe**

oldest: _____

_____

youngest: _____   [1]

b Draw straight lines to match each **type of body** to its **description**.

Type of body
moon
comet
asteroid
star

Description
a body that looks like a small, rocky planet
a natural satellite
a ball of hot gases
a lump of rock held together by ice

[3]

c 2000 years ago, a Chinese astronomer, Gan Dej, saw Ganymede, one of Jupiter's moons. He did not have a telescope or other optical instrument.

Suggest why it was easier to see Ganymede without a telescope 2000 years ago than it is now.

_____   [1]

d Use the information in the box and the table to answer questions **i** and **ii**.

> In August 2006, the scientists of the International Astronomical Union defined a planet as a body that orbits a star, is big enough to have a spherical shape, and has no other objects in its orbit. They also identified four 'dwarf planets', including Pluto.

Name of dwarf planet	Approximate diameter (km)	Object it orbits	Other information
UB313 (Xena)	3000	Sun	It was made from gases and dust when the Solar System began.
Pluto	2400	Sun	Its orbit overlaps Neptune's orbit.
Ceres	1200	Sun	It is the biggest object in the asteroid belt.

i Give one way in which UB313 *does* fit the definition of a planet.

_____

ii Give one way in which Pluto *does* not fit the definition of a planet.

_____   [2]

Total [7]

2 a On the diagram of the Earth, label the **crust**, **mantle**, and **core**.

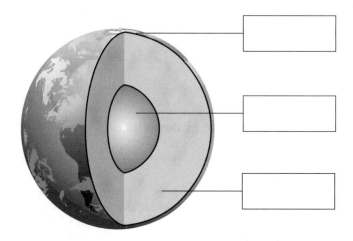

[2]

b Draw straight lines to match each **explanation** with **evidence** that supports it.

Explanation	Evidence
1 South America and Africa were once part of one big continent.	**A** Scientists have found many craters.
2 Mountains are being formed all the time.	**B** Radioactive dating of rocks.
3 The Earth is older than four thousand million years.	**C** Scientists have found the same fossils on both sides of the Atlantic Ocean.
4 Asteroids have collided with Earth.	**D** Rocks are continually eroded but the continents are not all at sea level.

[3]

Total [5]

3 In the year 964, a Persian astronomer called Abd al-Rahman al-Sufi described Andromeda galaxy. He noticed that it gave out light.

a Give the name of the galaxy of which our Solar System is a part.

_____

[1]

b How many stars are there in a typical galaxy?
Put a ring round the correct answer.

thousands of millions   **about a million**

millions of millions   **about a thousand**

[1]

c Why does Andromeda galaxy give out light?
Put a tick in the box next to the best answer.

There are many planets in Andromeda. These give out light. ☐

There are many moons in Andromeda. These give out light. ☐

Andromeda reflects light from our Sun. ☐

The stars of Andromeda emit light. ☐ [1]

d Abd al-Rahman al-Sufi recorded the positions and colours of some of Andromeda's stars.

i Why are the stars different colours?

_____

_____

_____ [1]

ii Today, scientists still cannot be certain of the distances of stars and galaxies from Earth.
Put ticks in the boxes next to the **best two** reasons for this uncertainty.

Everything we know about stars and galaxies comes only from the radiation they emit. ☐

Scientists use a star's relative brightness to measure its distance from Earth. But relative brightness also depends on how much dust there is between the star and the Earth. ☐

Scientists use a star's relative brightness to measure its distance from Earth. But relative brightness also depends on what stage in its life cycle a star is at. ☐

It is impossible to measure distances when it is cloudy. ☐ [2]

iii The distance from Andromeda to Earth is approximately 2 million light-years.

What is a light-year?

_____

_____ [1]

Total [7]

H **4** **a** At what rate do seafloors spread?
Put a ring round the best answer.

1 cm/year **10 cm/year** **1 m/year** **1 km/year** [1]

b Put the letters of the statements in the box in a sensible order to create a paragraph that describes and explains an observation.

_____ because _____ and _____.

> **A** the Earth's magnetic field reverses regularly
>
> **B** there is a symmetrical pattern in the magnetism recorded on either side of oceanic ridges
>
> **C** magma erupts, cools, and solidifies at the middle of oceanic ridges

[1]

c Draw straight lines to match each **event** with **how it happens**.

Event	How it happens
1 Mountain building	**A** Magma comes out of a hole in the Earth's surface at a place where the crust is being made or destroyed.
2 Earthquakes	**B** Tectonic plates move towards each other and collide. Massive pressure makes the rocks fold over on top of each other.
3 Volcanoes	**C** Blocks of rock on either side of a fault move. Pressure builds up and the rocks eventually snap.

[2]

Total [4]

1 Add the names of the missing electromagnetic radiations.

radio waves		infrared		ultraviolet		gamma rays

increasing energy ⟶

2 Write each of these electromagnetic radiations in the correct column of the table.

ultraviolet   **light**   **X-rays**   **infrared**
          gamma rays   **microwaves**

Ionizing radiations	Radiations that cause a heating effect only

3 Use the words in the box to finish labelling the diagram.

detector   energy of one photon   intensity   source
absorbs   number of photons   transmits   reflects

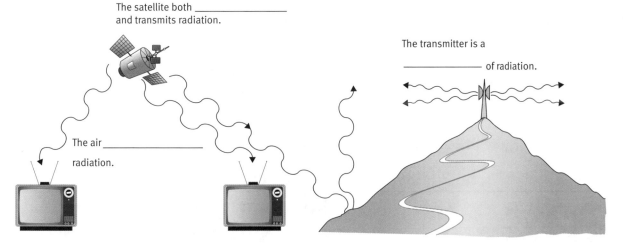

The satellite both _____ and transmits radiation.

The transmitter is a

_____ of radiation.

The air _____ radiation.

The TV is a _____ .

It _____ radiation.
The energy deposited here by a beam of radiation

depends on the _____

and the _____ .

The hill _____ radiation.

The energy that arrives at a surface each second

is the _____ of the radiation.

4 Add captions to each picture. Include

- ▮ the name of the type of electromagnetic radiation represented (radio waves, ultraviolet radiation, and so on)
- ▮ the damage (if any) this type of radiation can do to living cells
- ▮ what Alex can do to protect himself from this type of radiation (if he needs to do anything)

Alex's holiday: a day in the life

(Picture 3 speech bubble: Is that the dentist? My filling's just fallen out.)

5 Solve the anagrams in the box.

Then use the words to fill in the gaps.

camel chi	its ninety	i noizing	rat vibe	acne riots	emit

_____ radiation breaks particles into ions,

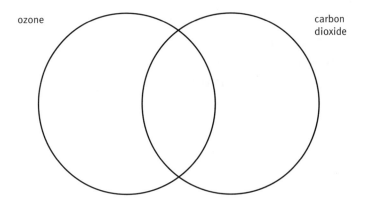 which can then take part in other _____ _____.

Non-ionizing radiations can heat the materials they strike by

making their particles _____. The heating

effect depends on the radiation's _____

and the length of _____ it strikes the material.

6 Write each letter in the correct section of the diagram.

A This gas is added to the atmosphere by respiration.

B This gas is made in the atmosphere when oxygen molecules absorb ultraviolet radiation.

C This gas is removed from the atmosphere in a chemical process that involves the absorption of ultraviolet radiation.

D This gas is present in the Earth's atmosphere.

E This gas helps to prevent humans getting skin cancer.

F Molecules of this gas contain at least two oxygen atoms.

G This gas is removed from the atmosphere by photosynthesis.

H This gas is added to the atmosphere by combustion.

I This gas absorbs radiation that the Earth emits, so keeping the Earth warmer than it would otherwise be.

J This gas helps to prevent humans getting eye cataracts.

ozone   carbon dioxide

What is radiation?

Radiation

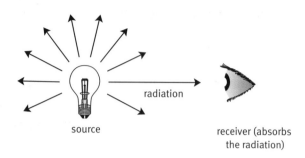

- carries energy
- spreads out (radiates) from its source
- may be detected by a receiver; receivers absorb the radiation

source

radiation

receiver (absorbs the radiation)

On its journey, radiation is reflected, transmitted, or absorbed by other materials.

How much energy does electromagnetic radiation deliver?

Electromagnetic radiation delivers energy in packets, or **photons**. The amount of energy delivered to a receiver depends on

- the number of photons that arrive
- how much energy each photon carries

The **intensity** of electromagnetic radiation is the energy that arrives at a surface in one second. The further the surface is from a source, the lower the intensity of radiation that hits it.

H This is because radiation spreads out as it gets further from the source.

What do different types of electromagnetic radiation do?

The electromagnetic spectrum includes these radiations:

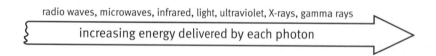

radio waves, microwaves, infrared, light, ultraviolet, X-rays, gamma rays

increasing energy delivered by each photon

Ultraviolet radiation, X-rays, and gamma rays are **ionizing radiations**. They break particles into ions that then can take part in other chemical reactions.

Radio waves, microwaves, light, and infrared radiation can **heat** materials by making their particles vibrate faster. The heating effect depends on the radiation's intensity
H and the length of time it strikes the material.

Some radiations are used to **transmit information**:

- Radio waves broadcast radio and TV programmes.
- Microwaves send messages between mobile phones and phone masts.
- Infrared radiation sends messages between remote controls and TVs.

What harm does electromagnetic radiation do?

▶ **Ionizing radiation:**
   – Large amounts kill cells.
   – Small amounts damage a cell's DNA. The cell may then grow uncontrollably to form a cancer tumour.
▶ The **heating effect** of absorbed radiation can damage cells.
▶ **Low-intensity microwave radiation** from mobile phone masts and handsets may be a health risk – scientists are not sure.

Barriers **protect** humans from radiation:

▶ Microwave ovens have metal cases that reflect microwaves to stop them leaving the oven.
▶ People wear clothes and sunscreen to absorb the Sun's ultraviolet radiation. These reduce the risk of getting sunburn or skin cancer.

How does electromagnetic radiation make life on Earth possible?

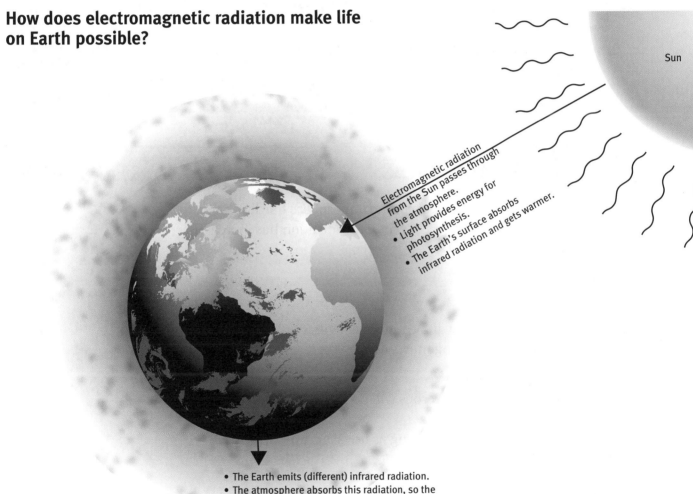

Sun

Electromagnetic radiation from the Sun passes through the atmosphere.
• Light provides energy for photosynthesis.
• The Earth's surface absorbs infrared radiation and gets warmer.

• The Earth emits (different) infrared radiation.
• The atmosphere absorbs this radiation, so the Earth is warmer than it would otherwise be.

This is the greenhouse effect.

What is global warming?

Greenhouse gases keep the Earth warmer than it would otherwise be.

There are three main greenhouse gases in the Earth's atmosphere:

▶ carbon dioxide (small amounts)

H ▶ methane (trace amounts)

▶ water vapour

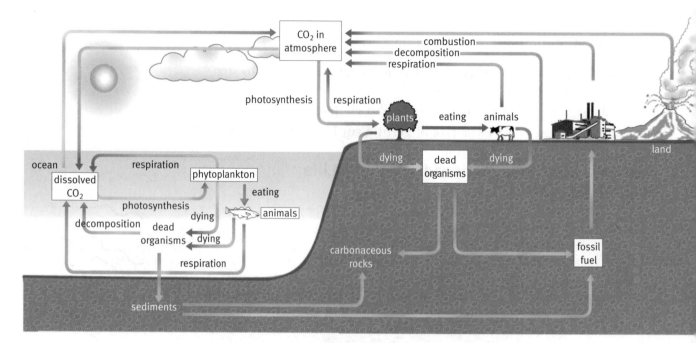

The concentration of carbon dioxide in the atmosphere hardly changed for thousands of years. But since 1800 its concentration has increased, mainly because humans

▶ burn fossil fuels for energy
▶ burn forests to clear land

Computer climate models show that human activities are causing global warming. Global warming may lead to

▶ extreme weather conditions
▶ climate change, so some food crops will no longer grow in some places
▶ ice melting and sea water expanding as it warms up, causing rising sea levels and flooding

What is the zone layer?

In the upper atmosphere, radiation acts on oxygen to make ozone. Ozone absorbs ultraviolet radiation and protects living organisms from its harmful effects.

1 a Draw straight lines to link each type of radiation with one of its uses.

Type of radiation	Use
infrared	broadcasting television programmes
microwaves	transmitting messages between phone masts
radio waves	transmitting messages between remote controls and televisions

[3]

b Add to the diagram of a microwave oven by finishing the labels.

Choose words from the box.

emits	absorbs	transmits	reflects

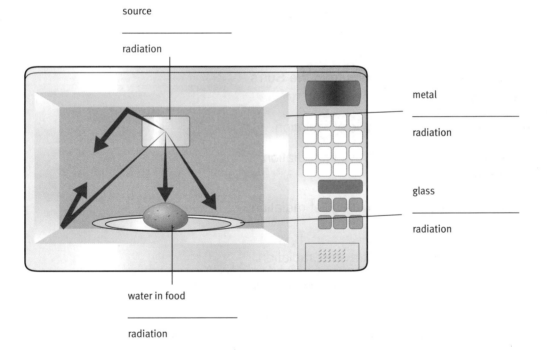

source

_____
radiation

metal
_____
radiation

glass
_____
radiation

water in food

_____
radiation

[4]

c Name one feature of a microwave oven that protects its users from the radiation it emits.

_____

_____

[1]

Total [8]

2 The Sun emits ultraviolet radiation.

a Ultraviolet radiation can be harmful.

Put ticks in the boxes next to the statements that are true.

Ultraviolet radiation is a type of ionizing radiation. ☐

Ultraviolet radiation makes molecules vibrate slower. ☐

Ultraviolet radiation can make cells grow in an uncontrolled way. ☐

Ultraviolet radiation makes molecules more likely to react chemically. ☐

Ultraviolet radiation can damage the DNA of cells. ☐

Ultraviolet radiation cools down molecules. ☐ [2]

b Name one physical barrier that people use to protect themselves from the Sun's ultraviolet radiation.

_____ [1]

c i Put a tick in **one** box to show how the Earth's upper atmosphere protects living things from the Sun's ultraviolet radiation.

Ozone molecules emit ultraviolet radiation. ☐

Ozone molecules reflect ultraviolet radiation towards the Earth. ☐

Ozone molecules transmit ultraviolet radiation in all directions. ☐

Ozone molecules absorb ultraviolet radiation. ☐ [1]

ii Some chemicals in aerosols destroy ozone molecules in the atmosphere.

Explain why many governments have banned these chemicals.

_____

_____

_____

_____ [2]

Total [6]

3 Beams of electromagnetic radiation from the phone mast deliver photons ('packets') of energy to Mike's and Helen's mobile phones.

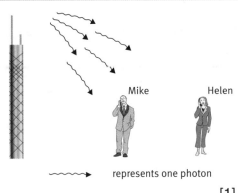

Mike   Helen

⟿ represents one photon

a The amount of energy delivered by each photon is the same. Explain why the amount of energy that arrives at Helen's mobile phone is less than the amount of energy that arrives at Mike's mobile phone.

_____

[1]

b The graph shows how the intensity of a beam of electromagnetic radiation changes as the distance from its source increases.

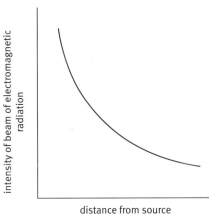

intensity of beam of electromagnetic radiation

distance from source

i Complete this sentence:

As the distance from the source increases, the intensity

of the beam _____.   [1]

ii Explain why the intensity of the beam changes in this way as the distance from the source increases.

_____

_____

[1]

c Complete these sentences. Choose words from the box.

intensity	vibrate	time	ionize	temperature

Electromagnetic radiation from the mobile phone makes Mike's

brain slightly warmer. This is because the radiation makes molecules

in the brain _____ faster. The size of the temperature

increase depends on the _____ of the radiation and

the length of _____ of his call.   [3]

Total [6]

23

4 The diagram shows part of the carbon cycle.

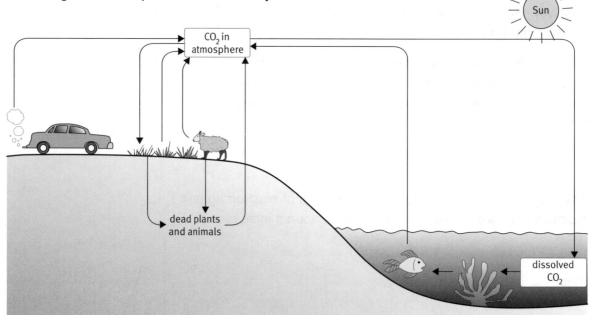

a i Name two processes that add carbon dioxide to the atmosphere.

_____ [2]

ii Name two processes that remove carbon dioxide from the atmosphere.

_____ [2]

b i Use the carbon cycle to explain why the amount of carbon dioxide in the Earth's atmosphere was approximately constant for thousands of years.

_____

_____

ii Give two reasons why the amount of carbon dioxide in the atmosphere has increased since 1800.

_____

_____ [3]

c Increasing amounts of carbon dioxide in the atmosphere cause global warming.

i Give two problems caused by global warming.

_____

_____ [2]

ii Name two greenhouse gases other than carbon dioxide.

_____ [2]

Total [11]

1 Draw arrows to link each label to one or both people.

A This person has breathed in a radioactive chemical. He is contaminated.

D Big doses of ionizing radiation kill cells.

B A radioactive source is irradiating this person.

E Smaller doses of ionizing radiation can damage the DNA in cells.

C Ionizing radiation will stop hitting body cells
  ▶ either when the radioactivity of the source decreases to zero
  ▶ or when the source is removed from body

F Ionizing radiation stops hitting body cells when he moves away from the source.

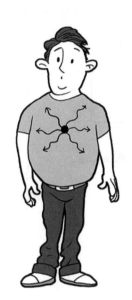

2 Solve the anagrams.

Use your answers to fill in the gaps. Use one word twice.

iznogini	**mad age**	**illk**
run dog	**paces**	**chill my ace**
stoma	**men tatter**	**mad lice**

We are exposed to _____ radiation all the time. Natural

sources of this radiation include radon gas from the _____

and cosmic rays from _____. Food and drink also

contain radioactive _____. Some people are exposed to

this type of radiation during _____ _____

or at work.

When _____ radiation hits cells it changes them and

makes them more likely to react _____.

Big doses _____ cells. Smaller doses _____

the DNA in cells.

3 Write each letter in an appropriate box to show how to generate electricity.

A heat up water to make steam

B wave movement

C tidal movement

D generator – a big coil of wire turns in a magnetic field

E solar voltaic cells

F releases carbon dioxide gas

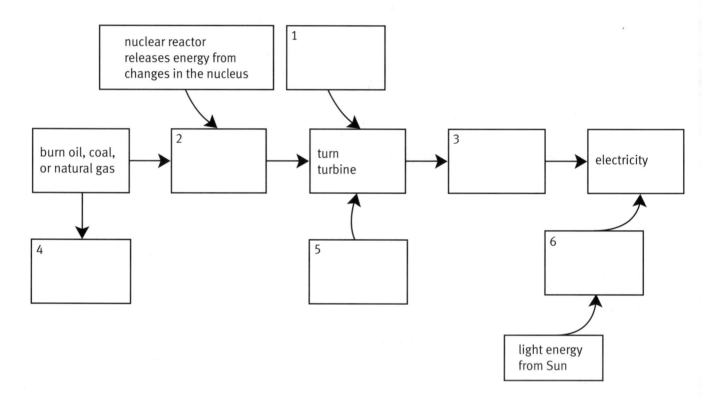

4 The data in the table is about electricity generated from different energy sources. Use the data to write one argument that supports each person's opinion.

	Nuclear	Wind	Coal
Approximate efficiency	35%	59% of wind's energy can be extracted by blades	35%
Environmental impact	produce radioactive waste	some people think they look unattractive	contribute to acid rain
Cost per unit of electricity (pence)	3.0–4.0	1.5–2.5	3.0–3.5
Tonnes of carbon dioxide made for one terajoule of electricity	30	10	260

Opinions:

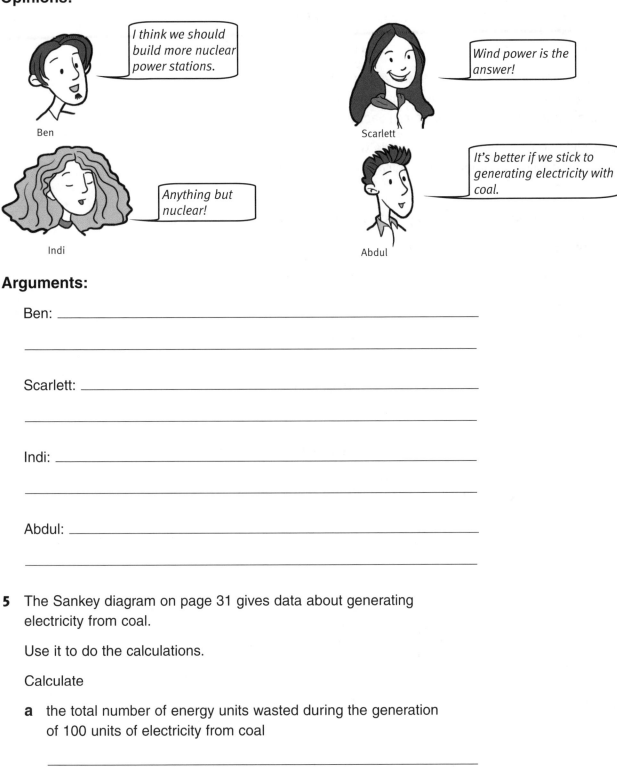

Ben

I think we should build more nuclear power stations.

Scarlett

Wind power is the answer!

Indi

Anything but nuclear!

Abdul

It's better if we stick to generating electricity with coal.

Arguments:

Ben: _____

_____

Scarlett: _____

_____

Indi: _____

_____

Abdul: _____

_____

5 The Sankey diagram on page 31 gives data about generating electricity from coal.

Use it to do the calculations.

Calculate

a the total number of energy units wasted during the generation of 100 units of electricity from coal

_____

b the efficiency of a coal-fired power station

_____

6 Write the letter **T** next to the statements that are true.
Write the letter **F** next to the statements that are false.

a Radioactive elements emit radiation all the time. _____

b Atoms of carbon-14 are radioactive. If a carbon-14 atom joins to oxygen atoms to make carbon dioxide, the carbon dioxide will not be radioactive. _____

c Solid caesium chloride that is made with caesium-137 is radioactive. It remains radioactive when it is dissolved in water. _____

d Alpha radiation is absorbed by thick sheets of lead. _____

e Gamma radiation can pass through a thin sheet of paper. _____

f Beta radiation is absorbed by a few centimetres of air. _____

g Radiation dose is measured in half-lives. _____

h Radiation dose is based on the amount and type of radiation a person is exposed to. _____

i About a million times more energy is released in a chemical reaction than in a nuclear reaction. _____

H **7** The diagrams show the number of protons and neutrons in six atoms.

A   B   C

D 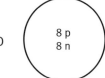   E 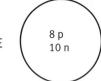   F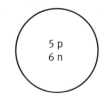

a Give the letters of two pairs of atoms of the same element.

_____

b Give the letter of the atom that has the fewest total number of particles in its nucleus. _____

c Give the letter of the atom that has the greatest total number of particles in its nucleus. _____

d Give the letters of two atoms that have the same total number of particles in their nuclei. _____

What are radioactive materials?

Some materials give out (emit) ionizing radiation all the time. You cannot change the behaviour of a radioactive material – it emits radiation whatever its state (solid, liquid, gas) and whether or not it takes part in a chemical reaction. Most radioactive materials are found naturally in the environment.

What types of ionizing radiation are there?

Type of radiation	What it is	Penetration properties
alpha	a particle	absorbed by paper or a few cm of air
beta	a particle	penetrates paper; absorbed by a thin sheet of metal
gamma	a high-energy electromagnetic wave	absorbed only by ▶ thick sheets of dense metals, e.g. lead ▶ several metres of concrete

Why are some materials radioactive?

Every atom has a tiny core, or **nucleus**. The nucleus is surrounded by **electrons**.

H The nucleus is made of **protons** and **neutrons**. Every atom of a certain element has the same number of protons. Different atoms of this element may have different numbers of neutrons. For example:

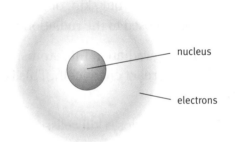
nucleus
electrons

Name	Number of protons	Number of neutrons	Is this type of carbon radioactive?
carbon-12	6	6	no
carbon-14	6	8	yes

The nucleus of a carbon-12 atom is stable. It is not radioactive.

The nucleus of a carbon-14 atom is unstable. It decays to make a stable nucleus of another element, nitrogen-14. As it decays, it emits beta and gamma radiation.

Other elements have atoms with unstable nuclei, for example radium-226. When radium-226 decays, it emits alpha and gamma radiation to make an atom of radon-222.

How does a material's radioactivity change with time?

As a radioactive material decays, it contains fewer and fewer atoms with unstable nuclei. It becomes less radioactive and emits less radiation. The time taken for the radioactivity to fall to half its original value is the material's **half-life**. Different radioactive elements have different half-lives. For example:

Radioactive element	Half-life
plutonium-242	380 thousand years
carbon-14	5.6 thousand years
strontium-90	28 years
iodine-131	8 days
lawrencium-257	8 seconds

What are the risks from radioactive sources?

We are exposed to **background radiation** all the time. Background radiation sources include:

▶ radon gas from the ground
▶ cosmic rays
▶ food and drink
▶ gamma rays from the ground and buildings

If ionizing radiation reaches you, you are **irradiated**. If a radioactive material gets onto your skin, or inside your body, you are **contaminated**. You will be exposed to the radiation as long as the material stays there.

When ionizing radiation hits atoms, it changes them. The atoms are more likely to react chemically. This is why ionizing radiation damages **living cells**:

▶ Big radiation doses kill cells.
▶ Smaller radiation doses can damage a cell's DNA. The cell may grow uncontrollably and cancer develops.

How is ionizing radiation useful?

▶ To **treat cancer**. In one type of **radiotherapy**, doctors put metal wires containing radioactive materials into the patient, near the tumour. The ionizing radiation damages cancer cells and they stop growing. However, the radiation also damages healthy cells.
▶ Gamma radiation kills bacteria on food and medical equipment, so **sterilizing** them.

How are radioactive materials handled safely?

The more ionizing radiation that a person is exposed to, the greater the risk of cancer. Some people are exposed to radioactive sources at work, for example staff in nuclear power stations and in hospital radiotherapy departments. Their exposure is monitored carefully.

Radiation dose measures the possible harm to your body. It takes account of the amount and type of radiation. Its units are sieverts (Sv).

How is electricity generated?

Electricity is easy to use and to transmit over long distances. It is a **secondary energy source** – it must be generated from another energy source, like gas.

Electricity is generated by these steps:

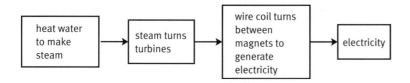

Generating and distributing electricity is not 100% efficient. At each step, energy is dissipated by heating the surroundings.

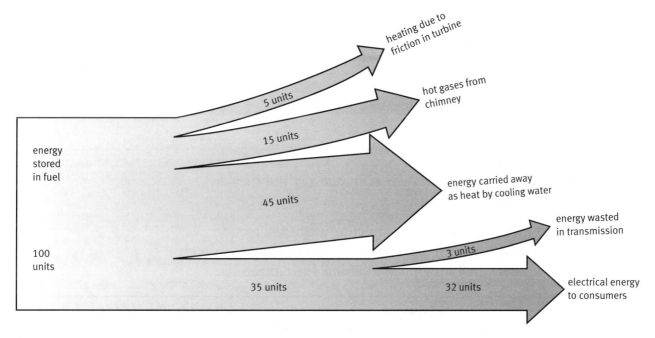

What are the energy sources for electricity generation?

▶ **Coal or gas**: burning coal or gas heats water to make steam. Steam turns the turbine. Coal- and gas-fired power stations make waste carbon dioxide.

▶ Generating electricity from **renewable energy sources** does not make carbon dioxide. These energy resources will never run out. Three examples are
   – Moving air turns **wind** turbines.
   – **Wave** movements turn turbines.
   – **Solar power** – photovoltaic cells generate electricity from the Sun's radiation.

⊞ How do nuclear power stations generate electricity?

Nuclear fuels release energy from changes in the nucleus.

They are used to generate electricity like this:

▸ **Fuel rods** in the nuclear reactor contain uranium-235.
▸ Neutrons are fired at the U-235.
▸ When a neutron hits a U-235 nucleus, the nucleus becomes unstable.
▸ The unstable U-235 nucleus splits into two smaller parts of about the same size – this is **fission**. At the same time, the nucleus releases more neutrons. Energy is released – about a million times more than in a chemical reaction.
▸ These neutrons hit more U-235 nuclei. Fission happens again. A **chain reaction** has started.
▸ **Control rods** absorb neutrons. They control the rate of fission reactions when they are lowered into or raised out of the reactor.
▸ Energy from the fuel rods is transferred as heat to a **coolant** (water or carbon dioxide).
▸ The hot coolant heats water in a boiler to make steam.
▸ The steam turns a turbine.

What happens to nuclear waste?

Nuclear power stations do not make carbon dioxide gas. But they do produce dangerous radioactive waste.

Scientists use half-lives to work out when nuclear waste will be safe. Elements that have long half-lives remain hazardous for many thousands of years; those with short half-lives quickly become less dangerous.

Type of waste	Example	How it's disposed of
low level	used protective clothing	packed in drums and dumped in a lined landfill site
intermediate level	materials that have been inside reactors – may remain dangerously radioactive for many years	mixed with concrete and stored in stainless steel containers
high level	concentrated radioactive material – decays fast and releases energy rapidly so needs cooling	difficult to store safely as radiation damages container; chemically corrosive

1 Read the article about treating cancer with radioactive materials.

> Arthur has a cancer tumour deep inside his body. His doctors will use radiotherapy to treat it. Arthur's doctors and radiotherapists plan the treatment carefully. They tattoo his skin to show exactly where to direct the radiation, and calculate the dose of radiation Arthur must receive.
>
> Arthur gets his treatment in a lead-lined room. When everything is ready, the radiotherapist leaves the room. Once outside, she switches on the treatment machine. Gamma rays enter Arthur's body for a few minutes. During the treatment, the radiotherapist watches Arthur on closed-circuit television. They can talk to each other over an intercom.
>
> Arthur goes to hospital for treatment every weekday for five weeks. On each visit, the gamma radiation enters his body at a different angle.

a i What type of material emits the radiation that enters Arthur's body?

_____

ii Why does the radiotherapist use gamma radiation, and not alpha or beta radiation?

_____

_____ [2]

b i What does gamma radiation do to cancer cells?

_____

ii Why is it important to direct the radiation exactly at the cancer tumour?

_____

_____ [2]

c i Why are the walls of the treatment room lined with lead?

_____

_____

ii Why does the radiotherapist leave the room while Arthur is receiving his treatment?

_____

_____ [2]

Total [6]

2 Caesium-137 (Cs-137) emits beta particles. It is used to treat some cancers.
The graph shows how the activity of this radioactive source changes over time.

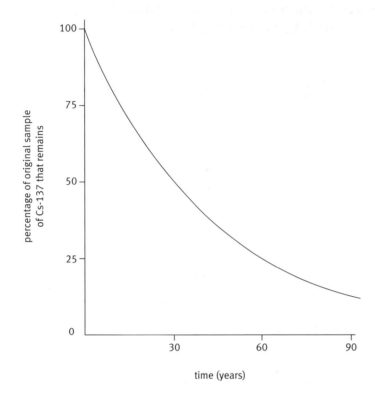

a Read the statements below.
Put ticks in the boxes next to each true statement.

The activity of the Cs-137 source decreases over time. ☐

Most radioactive elements have a half-life of between
10 and 50 years. ☐

The half-life of Cs-137 is 30 years. ☐

The longer the half-life of a radioactive source, the more
quickly it becomes safe. ☐

Beta radiation is absorbed only by thick sheets of lead
or concrete. ☐ [2]

b A sample of caesium chloride contains 10 g of caesium-137.

Calculate the mass of caesium-137 that will remain after 60 years.

_____

_____ [2]

H c Caesium-137 decays to barium-137. Barium-137 is not radioactive.

Complete the following sentences.

Use the words in the box.

negative	unstable	stable	neutral

The nucleus of a caesium-137 atom is _____. It decays

and emits beta radiation. This makes barium-137, which has a nucleus

that is _____.   [2]

Total [6]

3 a Nuclear power stations generate electricity.
The stages in this process are shown below.

A These neutrons hit more uranium-235 nuclei. Fission happens
again. A chain reaction has started.

B The steam turns a turbine.

C Energy from the fission reaction is transferred as heat to
a coolant, such as water or carbon dioxide.

D The unstable nucleus splits into two smaller parts of about
the same size. This is fission. At the same time, the nucleus
releases more neutrons.

E Neutrons are fired at fuel rods.

F When a neutron hits the nucleus of a uranium-235 atom,
the nucleus becomes unstable.

G The hot coolant heats up water in a boiler to make steam.

The stages are in the wrong order.

Write a letter in each box to show the correct order.

E	F					

[4]

H

b Complete the following sentences.
Choose from the words in the box.

barium	protons	electrons	boron
bismuth	neutrons	rate	

Control rods control the _____ of fission reactions

when they are lowered into or raised out of the nuclear reactor.

They contain _____ to absorb _____.   [3]

c Nuclear power stations produce radioactive waste.
Draw straight lines to match each **type of waste** to its
disposal method.

Type of waste
low level
medium level
high level

Disposal method
Mix it with concrete and store it in stainless steel containers.
Pack it in drums. Dump it in a lined landfill site.
Very difficult to store safely because the radiation damages the container.

[2]

Total [9]

1 Abdi is standing still.

Write one letter in each box.
Use each letter once, more than once, or not at all.

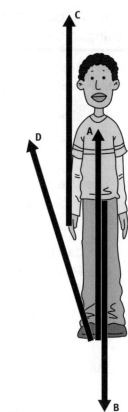

a Which arrow represents the force exerted by the Earth on Abdi? ☐

b Which arrow represents the force exerted by the floor on Abdi? ☐

c Which arrow represents the force of gravity? ☐

d Which arrow represents the reaction of a surface? ☐

2 Draw and label arrows to show the resultant forces on the rope, tricycle, and shopping trolley.

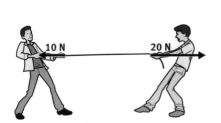
10 N   20 N

90 N
30 N

60 N
60 N

3 Faisal is moving a big loudspeaker.

Which caption belongs where? Write **A**, **B**, or **C** in each box.

A The friction force has reached its maximum.

B The size of the friction force is less than its maximum.

C There is no friction between the loudspeaker and the floor.

☐

I'm pushing really hard, but it's still not moving!
☐

At last! I've got it moving!
☐

4 David and Ruth are pushing on each other's hands. Neither person is moving.

Write **T** next the statements that are true.
Write **F** next to the statements that are false.

a The size of the force acting on David is less than the size of the force acting on Ruth. ☐

b The size of the force exerted by David is the same as the size of the force acting on Ruth. ☐

c David exerts a bigger force on Ruth than the force that Ruth exerts on David. ☐

d Ruth experiences a bigger force than David. ☐

e Ruth and David exert forces of the same size. ☐

f The force exerted by Ruth is in the same direction as the force exerted by David. ☐

g The forces exerted by David and Ruth are opposite in direction. ☐

5 a The statements below explain how the bike starts to move forwards.

They are not in the right order.

A The cyclist pushes down on a pedal.

B The wheels exert a backwards force on the road surface.

C The bike moves forwards.

D The wheels start to turn.

E The other force in the reaction pair is the forward force on the bike.

Fill in the boxes so the parts of the explanation are in a sensible order.

The first one has been done for you.

| A | ☐ | ☐ | ☐ | ☐ |

6 Saima pulls along her suitcase.

The arrows show the directions of the counter-force and the driving force.

Write **T** next to the statements that are true.
Write **F** next to the statements that are false.

a If the driving force is less than the counter-force, the suitcase slows down.

b Saima exerts the driving force to pull the suitcase along.

c If the driving force is equal to the counter-force, the suitcase moves with a constant velocity.

d The counter-force is caused by air resistance only.

e The counter-force is caused by friction and air resistance.

f If the driving force is more than the counter-force, the suitcase speeds up.

g If the driving force is equal to the counter-force, the suitcase cannot move.

7 Calculate the average speed of the following. Include units in your answers.

a A helicopter travels 600 metres in 3 minutes.

Average speed = _____

b A football travels 80 metres in 2 seconds.

Average speed = _____

c A racehorse runs 900 metres in 50 seconds.

Average speed = _____

d A worm moves 32 centimetres in 8 seconds.

Average speed = _____

8 Kelly goes shopping at the mall. On the right is a distance–time graph for part of her time there.

Label the graph by writing one letter in each box.

A Standing still to look at shoes in a shop window

B Walking quickly from the bus stop to the shops

C Walking slowly past some clothes shops

D Running at a constant speed

E Starting to run when she realizes she is late to meet her friend

F Slowing down when she sees her friend in the distance

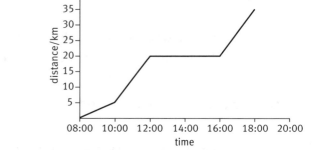

9 This is a distance–time graph for a whale swimming in the ocean.

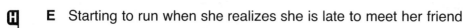

a Calculate the whale's average speed between 15:00 hours and 16:00 hours.

Average speed = _____

b Calculate the whale's average speed between 10:00 hours and 12:00 hours.

Average speed = _____

10 a Calculate the momentum in kg m/s of a 2000 kg sports car moving at a velocity of 44 m/s.

Momentum = _____

b Calculate the momentum of a 70 kg person on a 6 kg scooter moving at a velocity of 4 m/s.

Momentum = _____

c Calculate the momentum of a 9 kg baby crawling at a velocity of 1.5 m/s.

Momentum = _____

11 Pawel is a swimmer.

Here is his velocity–time graph for the first 55 m of a 100 m race.

Label the graph by writing one letter in each box.

A Pawel is waiting to dive in. He is stationary.

B Pawel is moving in a straight line. His speed is steadily increasing.

C Pawel has turned round. He has changed direction. His speed is steadily increasing.

D Pawel is moving in a straight line. He is swimming at a constant speed.

E Pawel is turning round. He is stationary for an instant.

F Pawel is moving in a straight line. He is slowing down.

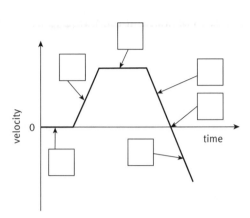

12 A driver does an emergency stop as a child runs out in front of her car.

The car stops in 3 seconds. The resultant force on the car is 5000 N.
Calculate the change in momentum.

Momentum = _____

13 Calculate the kinetic energy of each of the following.

a A 150 kg lion running with a velocity of 20 m/s

Kinetic energy = _____

b A 4000 kg bus moving with a velocity of 25 m/s

Kinetic energy = _____

c A 60 g tennis ball moving with a velocity of 44 m/s

Kinetic energy = _____

14 A monkey drops a banana. Its weight is 1 N. It falls 3 m to the ground.

   a Calculate the change in the banana's gravitational potential energy.

Change in GPE = _____

   b How much kinetic energy does the banana gain?

Kinetic energy = _____

   c What is the speed of the falling banana just before it hits the ground?

Speed = _____

15 Solve the clues to fill in the grid.

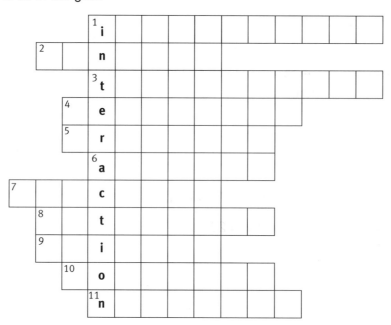

1 The two forces of an _____ pair are equal in size and opposite in direction.

2 A moving object has _____ energy.

3 Lorries and coaches have _____. These are speed–time graphs of the vehicle's motion over 24 hours.

4 Two people pull on a rope in opposite directions. The sum of the forces on the rope, taking direction into account, is the _____ force.

5 The force of _____ arises when you start pushing something over a surface.

6 Calculate the _____ speed of a car by dividing the total distance by the journey time.

7 A floor exerts a _____ force on a table leg that pushes down on it.

8 If you throw a basketball upwards, its gravitational _____ energy increases.

9 The force that makes you move forwards on a scooter is the _____ force.

10 Multiplying the mass of a train by its velocity gives you the train's _____.

11 If a football travels in one direction, its momentum is positive. When it moves in the opposite direction, its momentum is _____.

What are forces?

Interaction pairs

James and Wesley are arm wrestling. No one is winning – their arms are not moving. James's arm *exerts* a force on Wesley's arm. In return, Wesley's arm *exerts* a force on James's arm.

The arrows show the sizes and directions of the forces.

▶ Forces arise from an **interaction** between two objects. They come in pairs.

▶ Each force in an **interaction pair** acts on a different object. The forces are
  – **equal** in size
  – **opposite** in direction

Reaction of surfaces

Latitia is a fire-fighter. She is standing on a roof. Her feet push down on the roof. The roof pushes up on her feet with an equal force. This force is the **reaction of the surface**.

Resultant force

The **resultant force** on an object is the sum of the individual forces that act on it, taking their directions into account.

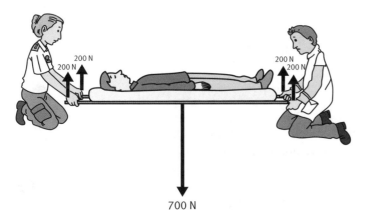

The resultant force on the stretcher is 100 N in an upward direction. So the stretcher starts moving up from the ground.

Friction

David tries to push a small skip that's blocking the road. The force of **friction** stops the skip sliding over the road's surface.

As David pushes harder, the size of the friction force increases. Eventually the friction force reaches its limit. Now the skip moves.

There was no friction force between the skip and the road before David tried to push the skip. Friction arises in response to the force that David applies.

friction = 2500 N

friction = 5000 N

friction at its maximum
(less than 6000 N)

The friction force balances David's push. The skip does not move.

The friction force balances David's push. The skip still does not move.

The skip moves. 6000 N is bigger than the maximum possible friction force for this skip and the road surface.

Getting going

Using friction

When you walk, you push back on the ground with your foot. The friction between your foot and the ground pushes you forward with an equal force.

If the surface is slippery you cannot push back on it, so the ground cannot push you forward.

When a car engine starts, the wheels turn. They exert a big backwards-pushing force on the road surface. The other force in the reaction pair – the forward force – is the same size. This gets the car moving.

If the road is slippery the friction force is small, so the car cannot move forward.

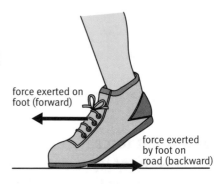

force exerted on foot (forward)

force exerted by foot on road (backward)

Rockets and jet engines

A rocket uses a pair of equal and opposite forces to get moving. It pushes hot burning gases out of its base, so the rocket is pushed in the opposite direction.

A jet engine draws air into its engine and pushes it out at the back. An equal and opposite force pushes the engine forward.

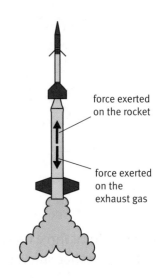

force exerted on the rocket

force exerted on the exhaust gas

Keeping going

Driving and counter-forces

Alex pushes Sam along on a skateboard. Alex exerts the **driving force** to push it forward. There is a counter-force in the opposite direction, because of air resistance and friction.

▶ If the driving force is **greater than** the counter-force, the skateboard speeds up.

▶ If the driving force is **equal** to the counter-force, the skateboard moves at a constant speed in a straight line.

▶ If the driving force is **less than** the counter-force, the skateboard slows down.

The driving force is equal to the counter-force.
The skateboard moves at a constant speed.

Speed and velocity

To calculate the **average speed** of a moving object, use this equation:

$$\textbf{speed (m/s)} = \frac{\textbf{distance travelled (m)}}{\textbf{time taken (s)}}$$

So if a dog runs 20 metres in 10 seconds, its average speed

$$= \frac{20\ \text{m}}{10\ \text{s}}$$

$$= 2\ \text{m/s}$$

Usually, the dog's speed changes as it runs. Its **instantaneous speed** is its speed at a particular instant, or its average speed over a very short time interval. Car speedometers measure instantaneous speed.

The **velocity** of an object is its speed in a certain direction.

Describing motion

Distance–time graphs

Distance–time graphs describe movement.

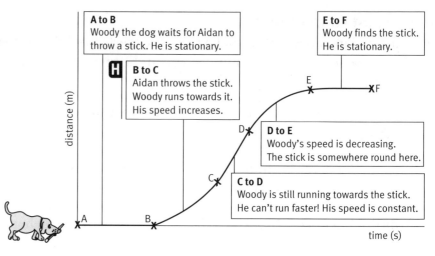

A to B
Woody the dog waits for Aidan to throw a stick. He is stationary.

H **B to C**
Aidan throws the stick. Woody runs towards it. His speed increases.

E to F
Woody finds the stick. He is stationary.

D to E
Woody's speed is decreasing. The stick is somewhere round here.

C to D
Woody is still running towards the stick. He can't run faster! His speed is constant.

H You can use distance–time graphs to **calculate speed**. The steeper the gradient, the higher the speed.

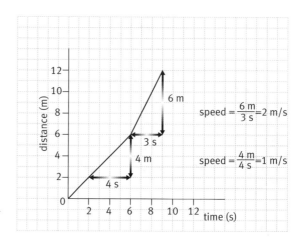

$$speed = \frac{6\ m}{3\ s} = 2\ m/s$$

$$speed = \frac{4\ m}{4\ s} = 1\ m/s$$

Velocity–time graphs

Velocity–time graphs show the velocity of a moving object at every instant of its journey. The graph shows the velocity of Ella, an ice dancer.

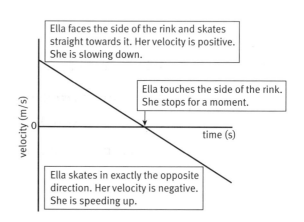

Ella faces the side of the rink and skates straight towards it. Her velocity is positive. She is slowing down.

Ella touches the side of the rink. She stops for a moment.

Ella skates in exactly the opposite direction. Her velocity is negative. She is speeding up.

Tachographs

Lorries and coaches have **tachographs** to record their motion. A tachograph is a **speed–time graph** of a vehicle's motion over 24 hours.

A speed–time graph is similar to a velocity–time graph, but does not show the direction of motion.

The connection between forces and motion

Momentum

All moving objects have **momentum**.

$$\textbf{momentum} \ (kg \ m/s) = \textbf{mass} \ (kg) \times \textbf{velocity} \ (m/s)$$

For a 0.5 kg bird flying at a velocity of 2 m/s

$$momentum = 0.5 \ kg \times 2 \ m/s$$
$$= 1 \ kg \ m/s$$

Momentum depends on direction. We choose a direction to call positive.

When the bird flies in this direction, its momentum is positive.

When the bird flies in the opposite direction, its momentum is negative.

Changing momentum

When a resultant force acts on an object, the momentum of the object changes in the direction of the force:

change of momentum = **resultant force** × **time for which it acts**
    (kg m/s)   (newton, N)   (second, s)

If a 3-second gust of wind from behind the bird exerts a resultant force of 10 N on the bird

$$change \ of \ momentum = 10 \ N \times 3 \ s$$
$$= 30 \ kg \ m/s \ \text{in the direction the bird is flying}$$

If the resultant force on an object is zero, its momentum does not change.

▶ If it is stationary, it stays still.
▶ If it is already moving, it continues at a steady speed in a straight line.

Road safety measures

If two cars collide, there is a change in momentum. When the cars stop, the momentum decreases to zero.

change of momentum = resultant force × time for which the force acts

Rearranging the equation:

$$\textbf{resultant force} = \frac{\textbf{change in momentum}}{\textbf{time for which the force acts}}$$

So the greater the time for which the force acts, the smaller the resultant force.

Many road safety measures make use of this idea:

▶ Car **crumple zones** squash slowly in a collision. So the collision lasts longer and the resultant force on the car is less.

▶ **Seat belts** stretch in a collision. This makes the change of momentum take longer. So the resultant forces on people in the car are less.

▶ **Air bags** cushion people in a collision. They make the change of momentum take longer. So the resultant force on the person is less.

Describing motion in terms of energy changes

Work done

Barney takes his daughter to the park. He pushes the buggy with a force of 15 N. The force makes the buggy move. Barney is **doing work**.

work done by a force	=	**force**	×	**distance moved by the force**
(joule, J)		(newton, N)		(metre, m)

The park is 500 m away from Barney's house. So

work done by Barney on the buggy = 15 N × 500 m
                                  = 7500 J

Barney **transfers energy** to the buggy. His store of chemical energy decreases.

change in energy	=	**work done**
(joule, J)		(joule, J)

change in Barney's store of chemical energy from pushing the buggy = 7500 J

The moving buggy has **kinetic energy**. Kinetic energy depends on **mass** and **velocity**.

kinetic energy = ½ × **mass** × **(velocity)²**
(joule, J)   (kilogram, kg)   (metre per second, m/s)²

So the faster the buggy moves, and the greater the mass of the child in it, the more kinetic energy it has.

If Barney pushes with a greater force, he does more work and so transfers more energy. The buggy goes faster and its kinetic energy increases.

In fact, the gain of kinetic energy by the buggy is less than the energy transferred from Barney. Barney must also transfer enough energy to overcome air resistance and friction. This energy is lost to the surroundings as heat.

Gravitational potential energy

Catherine picks up her doll from the ground. The doll's **gravitational potential energy (GPE)** increases.

change in GPE = **weight** × **vertical height difference**
(joule, J)   (newton, N)   (metre, m)

The doll's weight is 3 N. Catherine lifts it 1 m. So

change in doll's GPE = 3 N × 1 m
= 3 J

Catherine drops the doll. It falls 1m to the ground. Its kinetic energy increases.

GPE lost = kinetic energy gained

So the doll gains 3 J of kinetic energy.

H To calculate the doll's speed as it falls, use the equation

$$KE = ½ × mass × (velocity)^2$$

Rearranging gives

$$velocity = \sqrt{\frac{2 × kinetic\ energy}{mass}}$$

$$= \sqrt{\frac{2 × 3\ J}{0.3\ kg}}$$

$$= \sqrt{20\ J/kg}$$

$$= 4.5\ m/s$$

1 A fire engine travels to a fire.

The graph shows its journey.

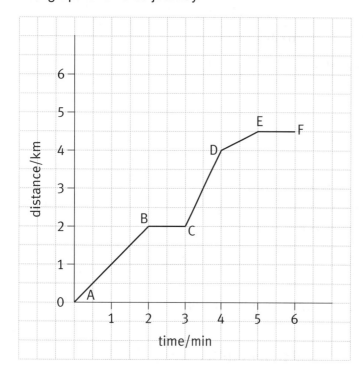

a i In which part of the journey was the fire engine moving along most slowly?

Draw a (ring) around the correct answer.

A to B   B to C   C to D   D to E   E to F   [1]

H

ii Describe the motion of the fire engine from **B to D**.

_____   [2]

iii Calculate the average speed of the fire engine between **A and B**.

Average speed = _____ km/minute   [2]

b A police car travels to the same fire.

It goes 6000 metres in 500 seconds.

Calculate the average speed of the police car.

Average speed = _____ m/s   [2]

c   An ambulance goes along a straight road to get to the fire.

   ▶   For the first 3 minutes its speed increases.
   ▶   For the next 2 minutes it moves at a steady speed.
   ▶   Then it slows down.
   ▶   It stops 7 minutes after its journey began.

Finish the velocity–time graph for the journey.

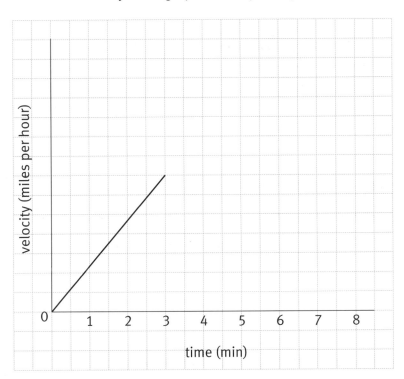

[3]

Total [10]

2 The picture shows a dogsled.

There is a heavy load on the sled.
The dog is trying to pull the sled forward.

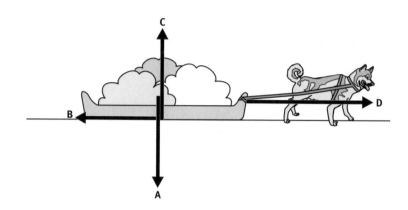

a Put a tick next to the row which correctly describes the forces on the sled.

A = gravity   **B** = reaction of surface   **C** = friction   **D** = pull of dog   ☐

A = reaction of surface   **B** = friction   **C** = gravity   **D** = pull of dog   ☐

A = gravity   **B** = friction   **C** = reaction of surface   **D** = pull of dog   ☐   [1]

b A person sits on top of the load on the sled.

What happens to the size of the force exerted by the ground on the sled?

Draw a ⟨ring⟩ around the correct answer.

increases   **decreases**   **stays the same**   [1]

c The dog pulls the sled at a steady speed.

The arrows show some of forces acting on the sled.

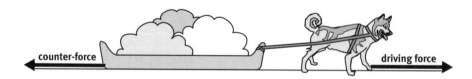

Which statement about these forces is true?

Put a tick in the correct box.

The counter-force is bigger than the driving force.   ☐

The counter-force is smaller than the driving force.   ☐

The counter-force and driving force are equal.   ☐   [1]

Total [3]

3 A penguin stands at the top of a slope. It slides to the bottom.

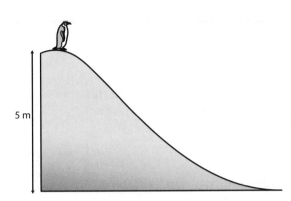

5 m

a i As the penguin slides down the slope its gravitational potential energy (GPE) and its kinetic energy (KE) change.

Tick the statements that are true.

The GPE of the penguin at the top of the slope is less than its GPE at the bottom. ☐

As the penguin slides down the slope, it loses GPE. ☐

The force of gravity does work on the penguin as it slides down the slope. ☐

The penguin's velocity increases as it slides down the slope. ☐

As the penguin slides down the slope, it gains KE. ☐ [2]

ii Calculate the change in the penguin's gravitational potential energy.

The weight of the penguin is 300 N.

Change in GPE = _____ J [2]

iii Assume that friction is small enough to ignore.

What is the change in the penguin's kinetic energy?

Change in KE = _____ J [1]

b A baby penguin travels down the same slope.

Its mass is 6 kg.

Its velocity at the bottom of the slope is 10 m/s.

Calculate the kinetic energy of the baby penguin at the bottom of the slope.

KE = _____ J [2]

Total [7]

4 A car has a mass of 900 kg. It is moving at 18 m/s.

   a Calculate the momentum of the car.

Momentum = _____ kg m/s   [2]

   b The driver is drunk. He crashes the car into a wall.

      The collision lasts 0.01 seconds.

      Calculate the force exerted on the car during the collision.

      Use the equation

      change of momentum = resultant force × time for which it acts

Force = _____ N   [2]

   c The driver was not wearing a seatbelt.

      How do seatbelts help to reduce serious injury?

      Tick the statements that are true.

        Seatbelts stop you moving forward in a crash. ☐

        Seatbelts stretch during a collision. ☐

        Seatbelts make the change of momentum of the driver
happen more quickly. ☐

        Seatbelts reduce the force that the driver experiences. ☐

        Seatbelts make you move forward more slowly during
a collision. ☐   [2]

Total [6]

5 Jack works in a supermarket. He pushes trolleys back to the shop.

   a Jack pushes the trolleys with a force of 300 N for 150 m.
Calculate the work done.

Answer = _____   [2]

   b What is the change in Jack's store of chemical energy?

Answer = _____   [2]

Total [4]

1 Use these words to fill in the gaps.

electrons	negatively	attractive	repel	negative	positive

If you rub a balloon on your jumper, the balloon becomes charged. _____

have moved from your jumper to the balloon. Electrons are _____ charged.

So now the balloon has a _____ charge and your jumper has a

_____ charge.

If you hold the charged balloon close to your jumper, it tries to move towards your

jumper. This is because there are _____ forces between objects with

opposite charges.

If you hold two balloons with the same charge close to each other, they try to move

apart. This is because like charges _____.

2 Draw lines to join the beginnings of the sentences to the endings.

Draw one or more lines from each beginning.

Beginnings
All conductors . . .
Insulators . . .
Metal conductors . . .
In a complete circuit . . .

Endings
do not conduct electricity
include polythene, wood and rubber
charges are not used up
the battery makes free charges flow in a continuous loop
contain charges that are free to move
contain electrons that are free to move
do not contain charges that are free to move

3 Draw a (ring) round the correct bold words.

Resistors get **colder / hotter** when electric current flows through them. This is why

lamp filaments glow.

The effect is caused by collisions between **moving / stationary** charges and

moving / stationary atoms in the metal wire.

The resistance of a light dependent resistor (LDR) changes with light intensity. Its

resistance in the dark is **less / more** than its resistance in the light.

The resistance of a thermistor changes with temperature. Usually, the higher the

temperature, the **smaller / bigger** the resistance.

4 Fill in the empty boxes.

Component	Symbol
	(A)
voltmeter	
battery (or cell)	
power supply	
	⊗
switch	
light dependent resistor (LDR)	
fixed resistor	
	(variable resistor symbol)
thermistor	

5 In the six circuits below, all the lamps are identical.

For each pair of circuits, draw a (ring) round the circuit in which the ammeter reading is greater.

a

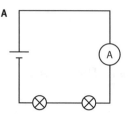

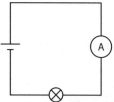

b

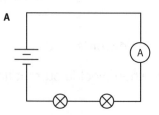

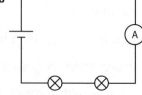

c

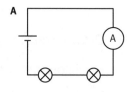

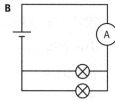

6 Write the letters of the statements below in a sensible place on the Venn diagram.

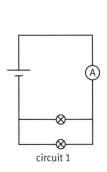

circuit 1

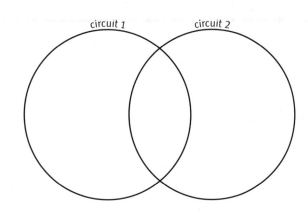

circuit 1   circuit 2

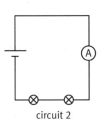

circuit 2

A The battery pushes all the charges through all the lamps.

B There are several paths for charges to flow along.

C This circuit has a greater total resistance.

D The ammeter reading is smaller for this circuit.

E The components resist the flow of charge through them.

F The total resistance is smaller for this circuit.

G The resistance of the connecting wires is so small that you can ignore it.

H It is easier for the battery to push charges round this circuit.

7 Calculate the resistances of the bulbs.

a

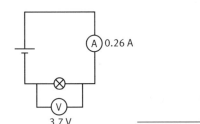

A 0.26 A

3.7 V _____

b

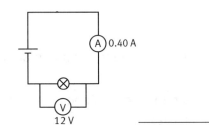

A 0.40 A

12 V _____

8 a In this circuit, the voltage is 230 V. The resistance of the fridge-freezer is 575 Ω.

What is the reading on the ammeter?

_____

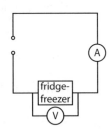

b This is the circuit in a simple torch.

What battery voltage would make a current of 0.5 A flow through the lamp?

_____

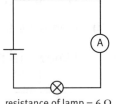

resistance of lamp = 6 Ω

57

9 Fill in the gaps.

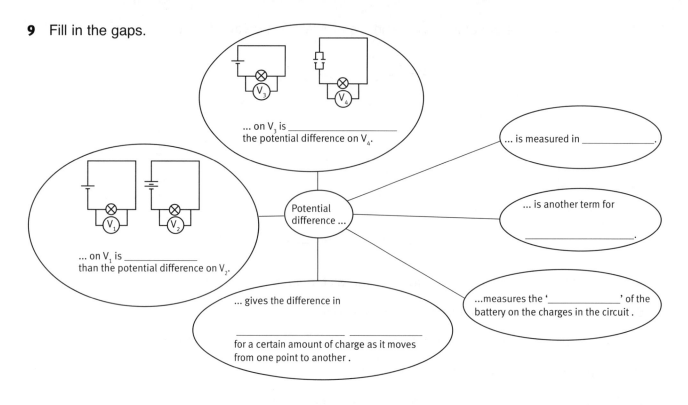

... on V_3 is _____ the potential difference on V_4.

... is measured in _____.

... is another term for

_____.

... on V_1 is _____ than the potential difference on V_2.

Potential difference ...

... gives the difference in

_____ _____ for a certain amount of charge as it moves from one point to another .

...measures the '_____' of the battery on the charges in the circuit .

10

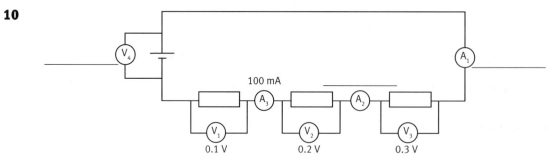

100 mA

V_1
0.1 V

V_2
0.2 V

V_3
0.3 V

a On the diagram, write the readings on ammeters A_1 and A_2.

b i On the diagram, draw a (ring) round the resistor that has the greatest resistance.

ii Draw a (ring) round the correct bold word below. Then complete the sentence.

The potential difference is **smallest / greatest** across the

component with the greatest resistance because

_____

c i On the diagram, write the reading on voltmeter V_4.

ii Complete the sentence:

I know that this is the voltage on V_4 because _____

_____

_____

11 Fill in the empty boxes. Use the right-hand column to work out your answers.

Appliance	Power rating (W)	Power rating (kW)	Time it is on for	Energy transferred (kWh)	Working
computer	250	0.250	2 hours		
kettle	1800	1.800	3 minutes		
toaster			5 minutes	0.10	
mobile phone charger			2 hours	0.04	

12 One unit (kWh) of electricity costs 10p.

Calculate the cost of using the following electrical items.

a A 1.9 kW washing machine for 1.25 hours:

Answer: _____

b A 0.5 kW surround sound system for 2 hours:

Answer: _____

13 Fill in the gaps.

If you move the magnet into the coil of wire, a voltage

is induced across the ends of the _____.

A _____ flows round the circuit.

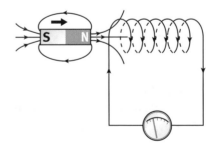

You can induce a voltage in the opposite direction by

moving the magnet _____ of the coil or

by moving the other _____ of the magnet

into the coil.

14 Calculate the current through these appliances.

The mains voltage in the UK is 230 V.

a A vacuum cleaner with a power rating of 900 W:

Answer: _____

b A DVD player with a power rating of 200 W:

Answer: _____

15 Calculate the voltage across the secondary coil.

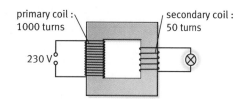

primary coil :
1000 turns

secondary coil :
50 turns

230 V

Answer: _____

16 Solve the clues to fill in the arrow words.

1 →								2 ↓	
3 →		4 →					5 →	
					← 6	16 ↓	
7 →							
8 →						← 9	
10 →						11 →	
12 →			13 →		14 →	
15 →							

7 Use this device to measure potential difference across a component in a circuit.

8 The symbol for the unit of resistance.

9 This device consists of a magnet rotating within a coil of wire.

10 Generators produce electricity by electromagnetic _____

11 The symbol for resistance.

12 Batteries produce _____ current.

13 This type of current reverses direction several times a second.

14 The symbol for the unit of electric current.

15 The percentage of energy supplied to a device that is usefully transferred.

Horizontal

1 Divide the voltage by the current to calculate this.

3 Home electricity meters measure energy transfer in

_____

4 The rate at which work is done by the battery on the components in a circuit.

5 The symbol for the unit of potential difference.

6 In this type of circuit, the current through each component is the same as if it were the only component.

Vertical

2 A flow of charge.

16 The abbreviation for direct current is _____.

Static electricity

If you rub a balloon in your hair, the balloon and your hair become charged. Tiny negative particles (electrons) move from your hair to the balloon.

Each hair is positively charged. Like charges repel. So the hairs get as far away from each other as possible.

There are attractive forces between opposite charges. So positively charged hairs are attracted to the negatively charged balloon.

Electric current

Electric current is a flow of charge.

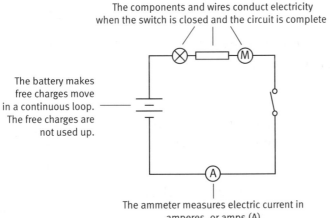

The components and wires conduct electricity when the switch is closed and the circuit is complete

The battery makes free charges move in a continuous loop. The free charges are not used up.

The ammeter measures electric current in amperes, or amps (A).

Metal conductors have many charges (electrons) that are free to move. Electric current is the movement of these free electrons.

Insulators do not conduct electricity. This is because they have no charges that are free to move.

Resistance

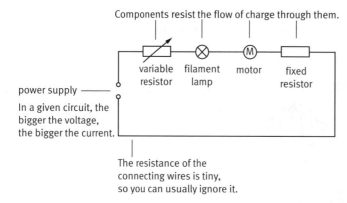

Components resist the flow of charge through them.

variable resistor   filament lamp   motor   fixed resistor

power supply

In a given circuit, the bigger the voltage, the bigger the current.

The resistance of the connecting wires is tiny, so you can usually ignore it.

For any circuit, the bigger the resistance, the smaller the current.

The current through a metal conductor is proportional to the voltage across it:

$$\textbf{resistance} \ (\text{ohm}, \ \Omega) = \frac{\textbf{voltage} \ (\text{volt}, \ \text{V})}{\textbf{current} \ (\text{ampere}, \ \text{A})}$$

The gradient of the graph is constant.

Resistors get hotter when electric current passes through them.

H This happens because moving electrons bump into stationary atoms in the wire.

Lamp filaments get so hot that they glow.

▶ Two resistors in series have more resistance than one on its own. The battery must now push charges through both resistors.

▶ Two resistors in parallel have a smaller total resistance than one on its own. There are now more paths for electric charges to flow along.

The resistance of a light dependent resistor (**LDR**) changes with light intensity. Its resistance in the dark is greater than its resistance in the light.

LDRs are useful for switching outdoor lights on at night and off in the morning.

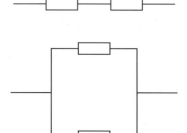

LDR

The resistance of a **thermistor** changes with temperature. For many thermistors, the hotter the temperature, the lower the resistance.

Thermistors are useful for switching water heaters on and off.

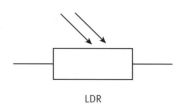

thermistor

current (A) — *voltage (V)* graph

Series and parallel circuits

The **voltage** of a battery shows its 'push' on the charges in a circuit.
Potential difference (p.d.) means the same as voltage.

Potential difference is the difference in potential energy, for each unit of charge flowing, between two points in a circuit.

Connect a **voltmeter** like this (see right) to measure the potential difference across a component:

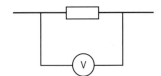

The readings on the voltmeter and ammeter are greater in circuit Y than in circuit X (see right). The second battery gives an extra 'push' to the charges in the circuit.

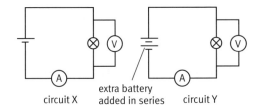

circuit X   extra battery added in series   circuit Y

H The readings on the voltmeter and ammeter are the same in circuits A and B (see right). The second battery in circuit B provides no extra 'push' to the charges in the circuit.

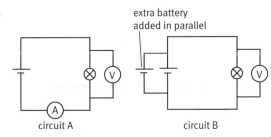

extra battery added in parallel

circuit A   circuit B

In circuit S, three components are connected in series to a battery. In circuit P, three components are connected in parallel to a battery.

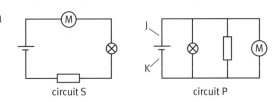

circuit S   circuit P

In circuit S . . .

- The same current flows through each component.

- The p.d.s across the components add up to the p.d. across the battery.

H This is because the work done by the battery on the electrons is the same as the work done on the electrons on the components.

- The p.d. is biggest across the component with the greatest resistance.

H This is because more work is done by charge flowing through a large resistance than through a small one.

In circuit P . . .

- The current at J, and at K, is equal to the sum of the currents through the components.

- The current is smallest through the component with the biggest resistance.

H The same battery voltage pushes more current through a component with a smaller resistance than through one with a bigger resistance.

- The current through each component is the same as if it were the only component in the circuit.

- The p.d. across each component is the same as the battery's p.d.

Electromagnetic induction

If you move a magnet into a coil of wire, a voltage is induced across the ends of the coil. This is **electromagnetic induction**. If you join up the ends of the coil to make a circuit, a current flows round the circuit.

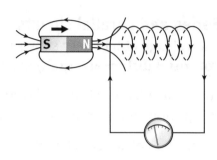

You can induce a voltage in the opposite direction by

▶ moving the magnet *out* of the coil, or

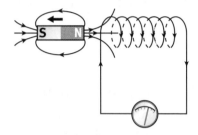

▶ moving the *other pole* of the magnet into the coil

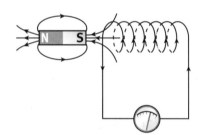

Generating mains electricity

Generators make electricity by electromagnetic induction. In a generator, a magnet or electromagnet turns near a coil of wire. This induces a voltage across the ends of the coil.

The direction of this voltage changes each time the magnet rotates.

rotate magnet

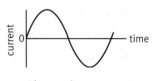

pivot

needle moves back and forth

You can increase the size of the induced voltage by

▶ turning the magnet faster
▶ increasing the strength of the magnetic field
▶ adding more turns to the coil
▶ putting an iron core inside the coil

Alternating current

H The magnet in a generator turns all the time. Its magnetic field constantly changes direction. So the direction of the induced current changes all the time. This is an **alternating current (a.c.)**.

The current from a battery does not change direction. It is a **direct current (d.c.)**.

Mains electricity is supplied as an alternating current (a.c.).

H This is because

▶ it is easier to generate than d.c.
▶ it can be distributed more efficiently, with less energy wasted as heat

current

0

time

Alternating current

Transformers

A transformer changes the size of an alternating voltage. It consists of two coils of wire wound onto an iron core.

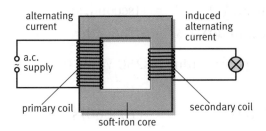

The voltage in the primary coil changes all the time. So it becomes a strong magnet. It induces a voltage in the secondary coil, where a current now flows.

H You can use this equation to work out the size of the voltage across the secondary coil:

$$\frac{\text{voltage across primary coil } (V_P)}{\text{voltage across secondary coil } (V_S)} = \frac{\text{number of turns on primary coil } (N_P)}{\text{number of turns on secondary coil } (N_S)}$$

The **National Grid** distributes electricity all over Britain. It uses transformers to change the voltage. Transmitting at very high voltage (so that the current is small) minimizes the amount of energy lost as heat.

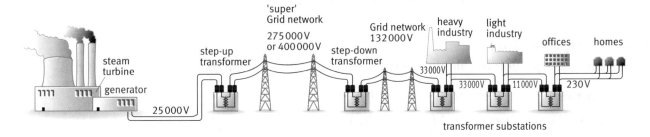

Electricity at home

Power

When electric current flows through a device, such as a computer, energy is transferred by the device.

The **power** of an appliance is the rate at which energy is transferred to it. Different appliances have different power ratings.

Energy transfer

You can use this equation to calculate the energy transferred to a device:

energy transferred	=	**power**	×	**time**
(joule, J)		(watt, W)		(second, s)
(kilowatt hour, kWh)		(kilowatt, kW)		(hour, h)

For example, Rashid uses a computer with a power rating of 250 W for 10 minutes.

$$\text{energy transferred} = 250\ \text{W} \times (10 \times 60)\ \text{s}$$
$$= 150\ 000\ \text{J}$$

Jason spends half an hour ironing shirts. His iron has a power rating of 3 kW.

$$\text{energy transferred} = 3\ \text{kW} \times 0.5\ \text{h}$$
$$= 1.5\ \text{kWh}$$

Paying for electricity

Home electricity meters measure energy transfer in kilowatt hours (kWh). One kWh is one unit of electricity.

$$\textbf{cost} = \textbf{number of units} \times \textbf{cost of one unit}$$

If one unit costs 10p, then the cost of Jason's ironing is

$$\text{cost} = 1.5\ \text{kWh} \times 10\text{p} = 15.0\text{p}$$

Current through appliances

You can use this equation to calculate the current through an appliance:

power	=	**current**	×	**voltage**
(watt, W)		(ampere, A)		(volt, V)

Ⓗ For example, the power rating of a hairdryer is 1000 W. The mains voltage in the UK is 230 V. Rearranging the equation gives

$$\text{current} = \frac{\text{power}}{\text{voltage}} = \frac{1000\ \text{W}}{230\ \text{V}} = 4.3\ \text{A}$$

Efficiency

You can use this equation to calculate the efficiency of an appliance:

$$\textbf{efficiency} = \frac{\textbf{energy usefully transferred}}{\textbf{total energy supplied}} \times \textbf{100\%}$$

For example, a 100 W filament lamp transfers 10 J of energy as light each second.

The total energy supplied by electricity is 100 J.

So the efficiency of the filament lamp is $\dfrac{10\ \text{J}}{100\ \text{J}} \times 100\% = 10\%$

1 Vanessa makes a model fire engine for her little sister, Ursula. She connects the circuit shown in the diagram.

When the switch is closed the lamp lights and the siren sounds.

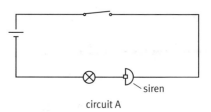

circuit A

a Which of the following statements are correct?

Tick each of the correct boxes.

When the switch is closed, the battery makes free charges in the circuit move. ☐

The metal wires contain electrons that are free to move. ☐

When the switch is closed, atoms in the light filament are free to move. ☐

Electrons are positively charged. ☐

When the switch is closed there is a flow of charge. This is an electric current. ☐

When a current flows in the circuit, free charges are used up. ☐

[2]

b Ursula wants the light to be brighter.

Vanessa connects these circuits.

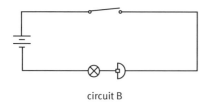

circuit B

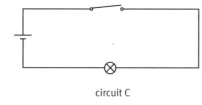

circuit C

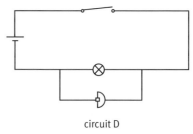

circuit D

In each circuit, the light is brighter than it was in circuit A.

Explain why, by choosing words from this list to complete the sentences.

voltage	current	resistance

The lamp in circuit B is brighter because the _____ of the

battery is bigger. So the _____ in the circuit is bigger.

The lamp in circuit C is brighter because the siren has been removed.

The total _____ of the circuit is less so the _____

is bigger.

The lamp in circuit D is brighter because there are more paths for the

charges to flow along. The _____ is bigger because the total

_____ is less.

[3]

Total [5]

2 Tamara has a portable heater. She plugs it into a car battery.

She puts the heating element into a mug of water to make a hot drink.

a Tamara wants to find out more about her heater.

She connects this circuit.

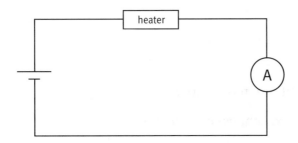

i Tamara uses a voltmeter to measure the voltage across the heater.

Draw on the diagram to show where to connect the voltmeter.

Use the correct symbol. [1]

ii The reading on the voltmeter is 12 V. The ammeter reads 10 A.

Calculate the resistance of the heater.

Resistance = _____ Ohms [2]

b The heater contains a heating element made from a coil of wire.

The wire gets hotter when an electric current passes through it.

Explain why the wire gets hotter.

_____

_____

_____ [2]

Total [5]

3 **a** Amir has a fridge-freezer. He leaves it on all the time.

Its power rating is 90 W, which is equal to 0.09 kW.

Calculate the energy transferred by the fridge-freezer in one year.

There are 8760 hours in a year.

Energy transferred = _____ kWh   [2]

b The French Environment Agency calculated that washing, tumble drying and ironing a pair of jeans every three weeks for a year transfers 240 kWh of energy as electricity.

The cost of one unit of electricity in France is €0.10.

Calculate the cost of washing jeans for a year in France.

Answer = _____   [2]

H **c** Over a year, an average British household spends £27 on running its washing machine.

One unit of electricity costs £0.10.

The power rating of an average washing machine is 1.10 kW.

Calculate how many units are used.

Calculate the total length of time for which an average British household uses its washing machine over a year.

Answer = _____ hours   [4]

Total [8]

4 The diagram shows part of an electric circuit in Matt's house.

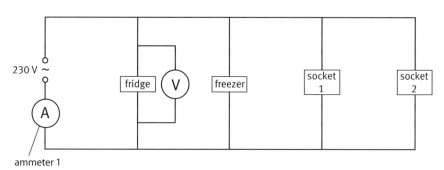

a i What is the reading on the voltmeter connected across the fridge?

_____

[1]

ii What is the potential difference across the fridge?

_____ [1]

b The resistance of the freezer is 70 Ω.

The voltage across the freezer is 230 V.

Calculate the current through the freezer.

Current = _____ amps [2]

c Matt plugs a kettle into socket 1.

What happens to the size the current through the freezer?

Draw a (ring) around the correct answer.

increases   decreases   stays the same [1]

H　**d**　Matt plugs a kettle into socket 1 and an electric heater into socket 2.

He switches off the freezer.

He measures the currents through the appliances that are switched on.

Appliance	Current (A)
fridge	0.4
kettle	5.0
heater	9.0

i What current flows through ammeter 1?

Current = ＿＿＿ amps　　　　[2]

ii Which appliance in the table has the greatest resistance?

＿＿＿＿＿＿＿＿　　　　[1]

H　Give a reason for your answer.

＿＿＿＿＿＿＿＿＿＿＿＿＿＿＿＿＿＿＿＿＿＿＿＿

＿＿＿＿＿＿＿＿＿＿＿＿＿＿＿＿＿＿＿＿＿＿＿＿　[1]

Total [9]

5 Scientists are developing a wind-up laptop computer. School students will use it in places where electricity supplies are not reliable.

A person turns a handle for 1 minute. This winds up a spring.

Then the spring unwinds slowly. This rotates a magnet within a coil of wire.

An electric current is produced.

a Suggest three changes the scientists could make to the generator so that it produced a bigger current.

Change 1: _____

Change 2: _____

Change 3: _____ [3]

b The computer can also be plugged into the mains electricity supply.

A transformer changes the size of the voltage.

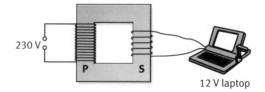

i Complete the sentences to explain how the transformer works.

Two coils of wire are wound onto an _____ core.

There is a changing magnetic field around coil P.

This _____ a voltage in coil S. [2]

ii Coil P has 2300 turns.

Calculate the number of turns needed in coil S so that the voltage across the computer is 12 V.

Answer = _____ [2]

Total [7]

1 Draw lines to match each type of wave to

- the direction of vibrations
- one or more examples

Direction of vibrations
vibrations are at right angles to the direction in which the wave is moving
vibrations are in the same direction as the moving wave

Type of wave
longitudinal
transverse

Examples
X-rays
sound waves
water waves
waves on a rope

2 Fill in the empty boxes.

Word	Definition
wave	
	The material that a wave travels through.
frequency	
	This vibrates to make a wave.

3 Draw and label two arrows on the diagram to show the wave's **wavelength** and **amplitude**.

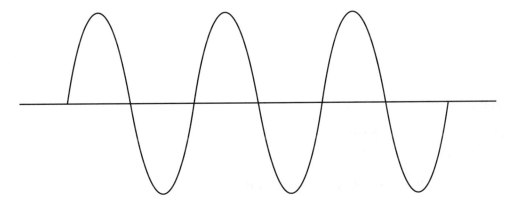

4 Calculate the speed of these waves. Include units in your answers.

    a A sound wave from a firework that travels 100 m in 0.3 seconds.

Answer = _____

    b A microwave that takes 0.000 033 3 seconds to travel from one mobile phone mast to another 10 km away.

Answer = _____

5 The diagrams represent water waves.

Write one word under each diagram. Choose from these words.

| reflection | digital | refraction | diffraction | interference | dispersion |

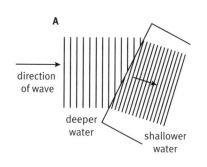

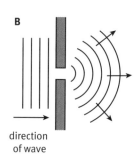

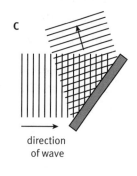

_____   _____   _____

6 Calculate the speed of these waves. Include units in your answers.

a Water waves in a swimming pool that are generated by a wave machine that vibrates once every second to produce waves of wavelength 2 m.

Answer = _____

b A sound wave from a bass guitar that has a frequency of 54 Hz and a wavelength of 6.3 m.

Answer = _____

7 Draw a (ring) round the correct bold words.

When two waves of the same frequency meet,
the effects of the waves add.

▶ If two waves arrive in step, they **reinforce / cancel out.**

This is **destructive / constructive** interference.

It is shown in diagram **A / B.**

▶ If two waves arrive out of step, they **reinforce / cancel out.**

This is **destructive / constructive** interference.

It is shown in diagram **A / B.**

H 8 Electromagnetic waves travel at about 300 000 000 m/s through space.

a Hannah wants to listen to a radio station that transmits 200 000 Hz.

What wavelength must she tune her radio to?

Answer = _____

b A TV satellite relays electromagnetic waves with a frequency of 500 million Hz.

What is the wavelength of the waves?

Answer = _____

9 Choose words from this list to fill in the gaps.

speed	slower	faster	wavelength	amplitude	refraction
frequency	reflection	away from	towards	diffraction	

Once a source has made a wave, the wave's _____ cannot

change. When a wave goes from one medium to another,

its _____ and _____ change. The wave

then changes direction. This is called _____. Light

travels _____ in air than in water. So when a light ray

travels from air to water it bends _____ the normal.

10 Add beams of light to the diagrams to show:

a Total internal reflection

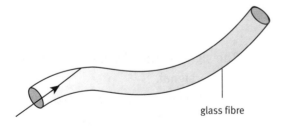

glass fibre

b Refraction

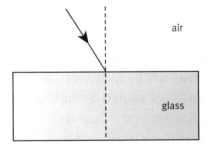

air

glass

c Dispersion

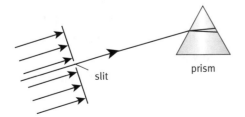

slit

prism

d Reflection

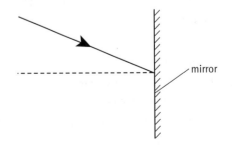

mirror

H 11 Complete the salesperson's speech bubble.

12 Solve the clues to fill in the grid.

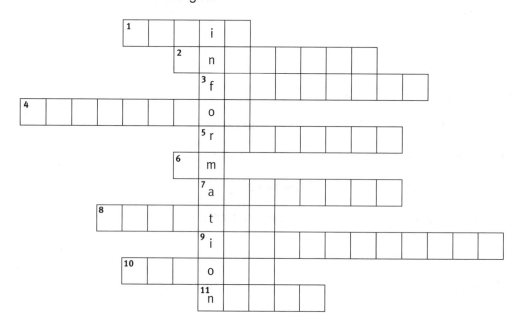

1 Signals are carried through space and the Earth's atmosphere by microwaves and _____ waves.

2 Signals are carried through optical fibres by light waves and _____ rays.

3 Waves that carry information must vary in amplitude or _____.

4 Information is carried by the pattern of a radio wave's _____.

5 A radio _____ decodes a radio wave's pattern of variation to reproduce the original sound.

6 The signal carried by FM and _____ radio waves varies in exactly the same way as the information from the original sound wave.

7 The signal carried by FM waves is called an _____ signal.

8 Sound waves can be converted into a _____ code made of two signals.

9 Analogue and digital signals pick up random unwanted signals as they travel. This is called _____, or noise.

10 Digital radio receivers pick up pulses and _____ them to make a copy of the original sound wave.

11 Digital radio receivers clean up signals to remove _____.

What are waves?

A wave is a disturbance that transfers energy in the direction the wave travels. Waves do not transfer matter. A wave comes from a source that **vibrates**. The material that a wave travels through is called the **medium**.

In a **transverse** wave, the particles vibrate at right angles to the direction of the wave's movement. Water waves are transverse.

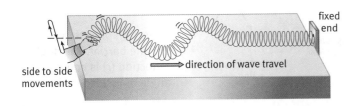

A transverse wave on a slinky spring

In a **longitudinal** wave, the particles vibrate in the same direction as the moving wave. Sound waves are longitudinal.

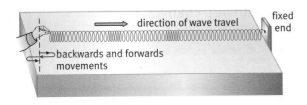

A longitudinal wave on a slinky spring

Describing waves

Frequency is the number of waves that the source makes every second. Its units are **hertz (Hz)**.

The diagram shows a wave's **wavelength** and **amplitude**.

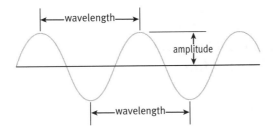

This equation gives the speed of a wave:

wave speed	=	**frequency**	×	**wavelength**
(metre per second, m/s)		(hertz, Hz)		(metre, m)

The frequency and speed of a wave are two separate things. For example, the speed of light in a vacuum is always the same, whatever the frequency of the wave.

Wave properties

Reflection

When waves are reflected, the angle of incidence equals the angle of reflection.

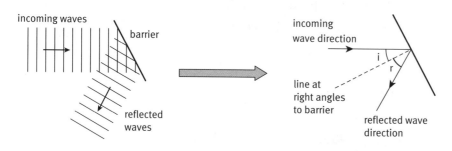

Reflection of water waves at a plane barrier. The angle of reflection (*r*) is equal to the angle of incidence (*i*).

Refraction

The speed of a wave depends on the medium. If a wave travels from one medium to another, its speed changes.

Once a vibrating source has made a wave, the wave's frequency cannot change. So when a wave's speed changes, its wavelength also changes. It may then change direction. This is **refraction**. The more the speed changes, the greater the direction change.

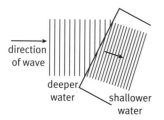

Refraction of water waves at a boundary between deep and shallow regions.

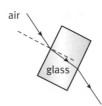

Refraction of a light ray when it enters and leaves a glass block.

Light waves travel faster in air than in glass. Imagine a light ray travelling through a glass block. It hits the glass–air boundary at an angle. If the angle of refraction for this ray would be greater than 90°, the ray is reflected. This is **total internal reflection**.

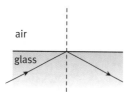

Light rays travel through optical fibres by total internal reflection. Optical fibres transmit telephone conversations. Doctors use optical fibre bundles to see inside bodies without cutting them open.

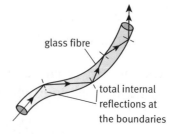

Diffraction

When waves go through a narrow gap, they bend and spread out. This is **diffraction**. The width of the gap must be similar to the wave's wavelength.

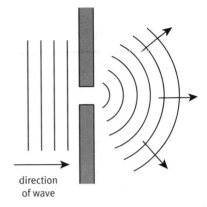

direction
of wave

Interference

When two waves of the same frequency meet, the effects of the waves add. This is **interference**.

▶ If two waves arrive in step, they **reinforce**. This is **constructive interference**.

▶ If two waves arrive out of step, they **cancel out**. This is **destructive interference**.

Two light beams of the same frequency interfere. They make a pattern of dark and bright patches. The dark patches are where the two waves have cancelled each other out. The bright patches are the result of constructive interference.

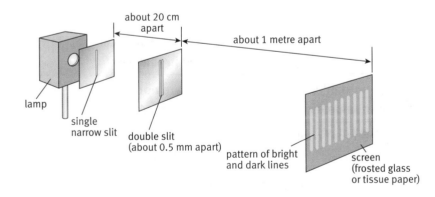

about 20 cm apart

about 1 metre apart

lamp

single narrow slit

double slit (about 0.5 mm apart)

pattern of bright and dark lines

screen (frosted glass or tissue paper)

Young's experiment. The double slits are two sources of light of the same frequency. Light from these interferes to produce a pattern on the screen.

Evidence for the wave nature of light

For many years, scientists were not sure how to think about light. Some scientists thought light rays were streams of tiny particles. Others believed light rays were waves. Evidence for the wave nature of light includes:

▶ Light rays **interfere**. They could not do this if they were a stream of tiny particles.

▶ Light rays can be **diffracted**.

Electromagnetic radiation

Electromagnetic waves consist of vibrating electric and magnetic fields.

Visible light is part of the **electromagnetic spectrum**. Different colours of light have different frequencies. The diagram shows the whole range of electromagnetic waves.

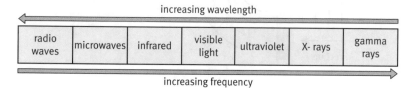

increasing wavelength

| radio waves | microwaves | infrared | visible light | ultraviolet | X- rays | gamma rays |

increasing frequency

All electromagnetic waves have these properties:

▸ They can travel through space. Space contains no matter. It is a vacuum.

▸ They all travel through space at the same, very fast, speed.

Electromagnetic waves transfer energy. The energy is emitted or absorbed in 'packets', called **photons**.

The photons of high frequency waves carry more energy than the photons of low frequency waves.

The **intensity** of a beam of electromagnetic radiation is the energy it delivers every second. Intensity depends on

▸ the number of photons that arrive each second and

H ▸ the amount of energy that each photon carries

Different frequencies of electromagnetic waves have different uses.

Type of wave	Use	Why the waves can be used in this way
radio waves	carrying information for radio and TV programmes	they are not strongly absorbed by the atmosphere
microwaves	heating food that contains water	they are strongly absorbed by water molecules
	carrying information between communications satellites and metal satellite dishes	they are reflected by metals they are not strongly absorbed by the atmosphere
light and infrared radiation	carrying information along optical fibres	they lose only very little energy when travelling through optical fibres
X-rays	taking 'shadow' pictures of bones or luggage	they are absorbed by dense materials, but not as much by less dense ones

Adding information to waves

Radio, TV, and telephone systems transmit information over long distances. Their signals can be carried by

▶ radio waves and microwaves through space and the Earth's atmosphere

▶ light waves and infrared rays through optical fibres

Analogue signals

The waves that carry information must be made to vary in amplitude or frequency. The pattern of variation carries the information.

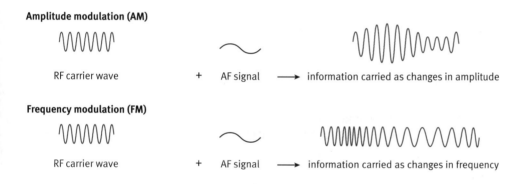

Amplitude modulation (AM)

RF carrier wave   +   AF signal ⟶ information carried as changes in amplitude

Frequency modulation (FM)

RF carrier wave   +   AF signal ⟶ information carried as changes in frequency

Radio waves travel through the atmosphere to a radio **receiver**. The receiver decodes the pattern of variation. It reproduces the original sound.

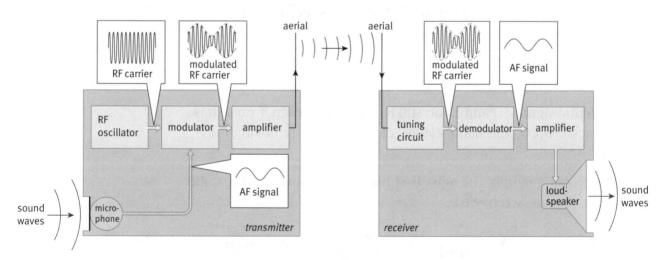

A simple radio system. When you speak into the microphone, a copy of the sound comes out of the loudspeaker. (RF is the radio frequency; AF is the audio frequency.)

The signal carried by AM and FM radio waves varies in exactly the same way as the information from the original sound wave. It is called an **analogue signal**.

Digital signals

Information is transmitted **digitally** like this:

▶ Sound waves are converted into a **digital code** consisting of two values (0 and 1).

▶ The digital code is transmitted as short bursts of waves, called pulses (0 = no pulse; 1 = pulse).

▶ Radio receivers pick up the pulses. They **decode** the pulses to make a copy of the original sound wave.

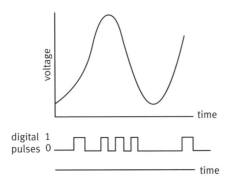

An analogue system and its corresponding digital pulses

Analogue and digital: which is better?

As analogue and digital signals travel, they pick up random unwanted electrical signals. This is **noise**, or interference.

Analogue and digital signals decrease in intensity as their amplitudes get smaller. So radio receivers must **amplify** the signals they receive – including any noise that has been added to the signal.

Digital signals transmit information with higher quality than analogue signals because

▶ with digital signals, 0 and 1 can still be recognized even if noise has been picked up. So the signal can be 'cleaned up' by removing the noise

▶ with analogue signals, the noise that has been amplified by the radio receiver cannot be removed

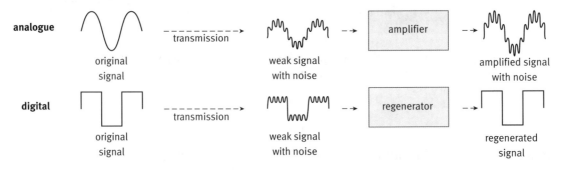

Digital signals can be 'cleaned up' by regenerators, but when analogue signals are amplified, noise gets amplified as well.

1   A new device helps hostage negotiators to track people's movements inside a room.

 ▶   The device sends radar pulses through the wall and into the room.
 ▶   Furniture and people reflect the radar.
 ▶   The device detects the reflected signals and analyses them.

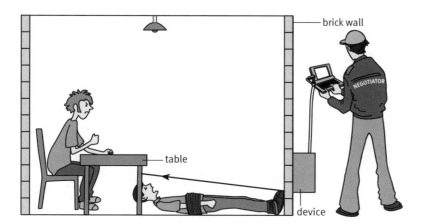

   a   Use a ruler to draw an arrow on the diagram to show the direction of the radar pulse after it has been reflected by the table leg.   [1]

   b   Radar pulses are microwaves.

      The diagram shows the electromagnetic spectrum.

      Which letter (A,B or C) represents microwaves? _____   [1]

   c   The device emits microwaves with a wavelength of 0.03 m.

      Microwaves travel through air with a speed of 300 000 000 m/s.

      Calculate the frequency of the microwaves.

                                              Answer = _____ Hz   [2]

   d   The device does not work if the wall is made from metal.

      Explain why.

      _____

      _____   [1]

                                                              Total [5]

2 There was an earthquake under the sea. Big waves moved through the sea, away from the centre of the earthquake. The waves were a tsunami. The tsunami caused great damage when it arrived at land.

a Scientists measured the tsunami waves as they arrived at a beach.

They made notes and drew a diagram.

Write down the amplitude, wavelength, and frequency of the waves.

Include units in your answers.

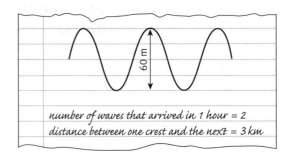

number of waves that arrived in 1 hour = 2
distance between one crest and the next = 3 km

▶ Amplitude = _____

▶ Frequency = _____

▶ Wavelength = _____ **[3]**

b The tsunami waves arrived at a big bay.

The entrance to the bay is 50 km wide.

The waves bent when they enter the bay.

i Draw on the diagram to show two waves in the bay. **[1]**

ii Give the name of the effect that happens at the harbour mouth.

_____

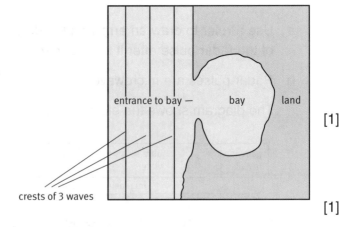

entrance to bay —   bay   land

crests of 3 waves **[1]**

c Near one coastline, the tsunami moved from deep water to shallow water.

The waves changed direction.

A scientist drew this diagram to show the crests of the waves.

i What is this effect called?

_____ **[1]**

ii Draw an arrow on the diagram to show the direction of travel of the waves in the shallow water. **[1]**

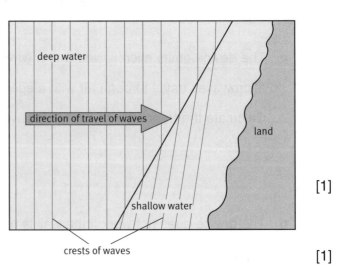

deep water

direction of travel of waves

land

shallow water

crests of waves

Total [7]

3 **a** The diagrams show different types of radio signal.

Draw a line to match each diagram to its description.

Diagram
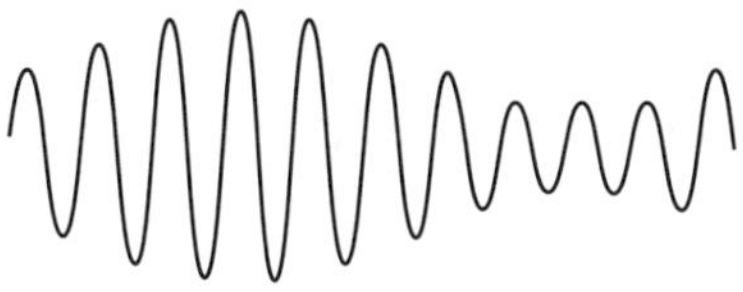
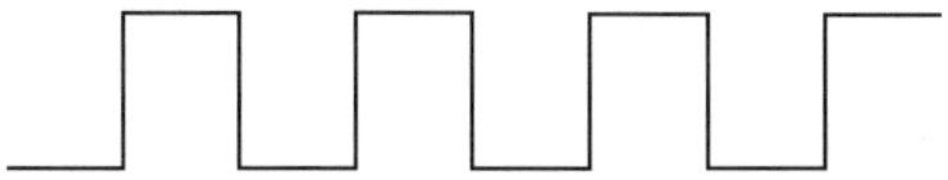

Type of signal
frequency modulated (FM)
amplitude modulated (AM)
digital

[3]

b The stages below show how radio programmes are transmitted and received digitally. They are in the wrong order.

A A radio receiver converts the digital electrical signals into sound waves.

B Sound waves are converted into digital signals.

C A radio receiver converts radio waves to digital electrical signals.

D Radio waves travel through the atmosphere.

E The digital signals are transmitted as a series of pulses.

Fill in the boxes to show the correct order.

☐ ☐ ☐ ☐ ☐

[4]

H **c** Explain why digital signals transmit information with higher quality than analogue signals.

_____

_____

_____

_____

[2]

Total [9]

4

Scientists have invented a scanner to find out if premature babies are at risk of brain damage.

The scanner sends beams of light into the brain.
It uses light of two wavelengths: 780 nm and 815 nm.

Some of the light passes through brain tissue.
Some of the light is absorbed by water in the brain.
Most of the light is scattered in all directions.

Detectors in the scanner measure the intensity of the light that comes out of the brain. If the intensity is less than expected, the baby's brain might be bleeding.

The scanner builds up a 3-dimensional image of the brain.
Doctors can use this to find out where the bleeding is.

a What scientific word means that light **passes through** brain tissue?

Draw a (ring) around the correct answer.

transmitted   **reflected**   **absorbed**   [1]

b Use the information in the box to decide whether blood transmits, reflects, or absorbs the light that the scanner emits.

Draw a (ring) around the correct answer.

transmits   **reflects**   **absorbs**   [1]

Give a reason for your decision.

One mark is for writing in sentences with correct spelling, punctuation and grammar.

_____

_____

_____

_____   [2 + 1]

c The diagram shows some of the detectors around a baby's head.

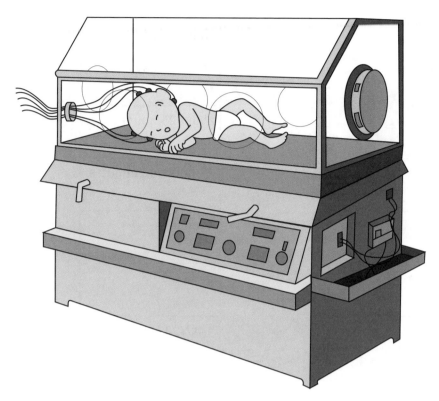

Each detector records a different reading for light intensity.

Why are the readings different?

Tick the **best** answer.

The amount of energy carried by a photon does not change. ☐

In one second, a different number of photons arrives at each detector. ☐

The amount of energy carried by a photon changes each second. ☐

Each photon carries the same amount of energy. ☐ [1]

d i Give one reason why it would not be sensible for the scanner to send X-rays into the brain.

_____ [1]

ii Give one reason why it would not be sensible for the scanner to send microwaves into the brain.

_____ [1]

Total [8]

1 Draw a line to match each description with the correct time period.

Description		Time period
time for the Earth to rotate once about its axis		about 28 days
time for the Earth to complete one orbit of the Sun		about 25 hours
a solar day		23 hours 56 minutes
time for the Moon to move across the sky once		4 minutes
time for the Moon to orbit the Earth		24 hours
difference between a solar day and a sidereal day		$365\frac{1}{4}$ days

2 Match the descriptions of the Moon with its appearance and position.

Look at the diagram (positions 1–8) to help you complete the third column.

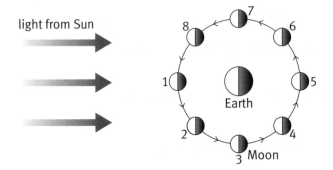

Position no.	Description	Appearance
		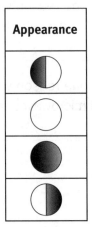
	full moon	
	new moon	
	first quarter	
	last quarter	

3 Draw a (ring) around the correct bold words.

▶ The **Moon / Sun** is a star at the centre of our **solar / constellation** system.

▶ The **planets / stars** orbit the Sun.

▶ It takes one **sidereal / solar** day for the Earth to rotate once about its **axis / orbit**.

▶ A **sidereal / solar** day is longer than this, since the Earth has moved further along its **axis / orbit** and it takes another **4 minutes / 28 days** before the same part of the Earth faces the Sun again.

4 Write **T** next to the statements that are true.
Write **F** next to the statements that are false.

a The Sun appears to travel across the sky from west to east. ☐

b During a solar eclipse the Earth comes between the Moon and the Sun. ☐

c Sometimes some planets appear to move backwards relative to the stars. ☐

d At night the stars in the northern hemisphere seem to move in circles about the pole star. ☐

e The Moon can only be seen at night. ☐

f In a lunar eclipse the Moon's shadow falls on the Earth. ☐

g The Sun is a star in the Milky Way galaxy. ☐

h Different stars can be seen at different times of the year. ☐

i Three angles are needed to pinpoint the position of a star at any particular time. ☐

j Eclipses of the Moon are more frequent than eclipses of the Sun. ☐

5 Arrange in order of size, smallest 1 and largest 6.

planet ☐   universe ☐   star ☐

solar system ☐   moon ☐   galaxy ☐

6 The diagram below shows the positions of the Earth and the planet Mars at intervals of one month.

a Draw straight lines to show the direction in which Mars is seen against the background of the fixed stars.

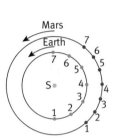

b Between which numbered months does Mars appear to move backwards?_____

c Mark an X on the diagram below to show the position of the Moon during a **solar** eclipse.

Mark a Y to show the position of the Moon during a **lunar** eclipse.

d Why do we not see eclipses every month?

_____

_____

_____

7 **a** Solve the clues to fill in the grid and find the mystery word.

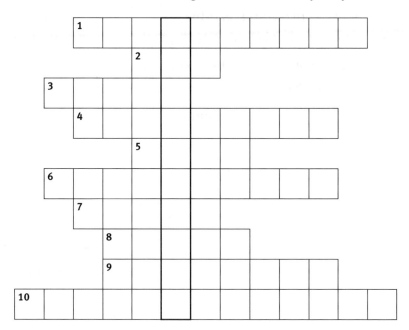

1 A scientist who studies the stars.

2 The colour of the Moon during a lunar eclipse.

3 The path of a planet around its star.

4 An ancient instrument for measuring the angle of a star above the horizon.

5 A natural satellite of the Earth.

6 The positions of stars were once used for this.

7 Area of total darkness in a shadow.

8 Word for a particular observed shape of the Moon.

9 The time taken for the Earth to rotate 360° is one _____ day.

10 A pattern of stars seen from the Earth.

b The mystery word in the grid above is used to describe the unusual apparent motion of some of word the planets. Write the word and its meaning.

▶ Word: __ __ __ __ __ __ __ __ __ __

▶ Meaning: _____

_____

What is the Solar System?

The Solar System is the collection of planets, comets, and all other objects that **orbit** the Sun. The Sun is a medium sized star.

The Earth takes 365 ¼ days to complete one orbit – we call this a **year**. It also rotates about an imaginary line called its **axis**.

H It takes 23 hours and 56 minutes for the Earth to make one rotation about its axis.

The Moon orbits the Earth. It takes about 28 days for one orbit.

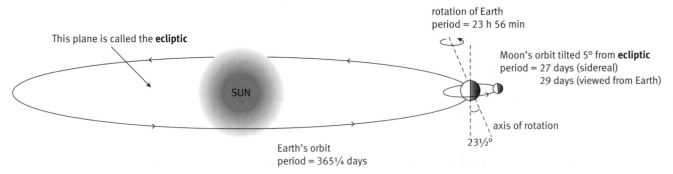

The orbits of the Earth and Moon (not to scale)

How do we measure the positions of stars?

The positions of stars and other astronomical objects are measured in terms of **angles** as seen from Earth.

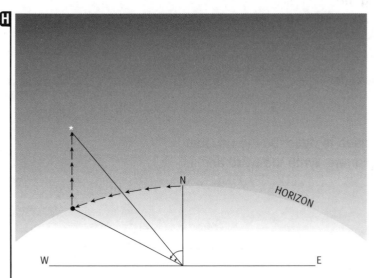

Two angles are needed to describe the position of a star.

One ancient instrument for measuring angles is the **astrolabe** – it was used for navigation.

Today scientists measure these angles to fractions of **seconds of arc** (where one degree is 3600 seconds of arc). Most stars are so very far away that their relative positions never change – they are called the 'fixed stars'.

Using an astrolabe to measure the angle of a star above the horizon

The movement of the stars

Long-exposure photographs show the stars to be moving in circles about the Pole Star. Of course they are not actually moving – we are observing them from a spinning Earth

The stars will appear to be back in the same places when the Earth has performed one rotation – almost 24 hours. We call this time a **sidereal day**.

The actual time of a sidereal day is **23 hours and 56 minutes**.

We can't see stars in the daytime because of the greater brightness of the Sun. We see stars only when the Sun is below the horizon.

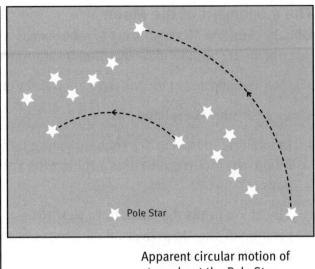

Apparent circular motion of stars about the Pole Star

A group of stars that form a pattern is called a **constellation**. We see different constellations in summer and winter because of the Earth's orbit around the Sun.

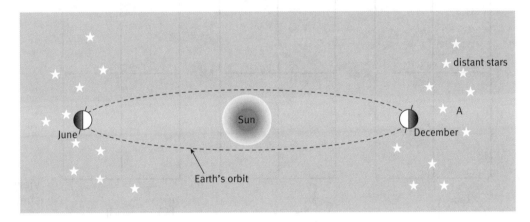

The distant stars at A can be seen in December but not in June.

The movement of the Sun

The Sun appears to move across the sky from east to west. It reappears in the same place once every **24 hours**. This is called a **solar day**.

The Earth spins round once in 23 hours and 56 minutes. During this time it has also moved further along its orbit around the Sun. For the same part to face the Sun again, it needs to turn for a further four minutes. This explains why a solar day is four minutes longer than a sidereal day.

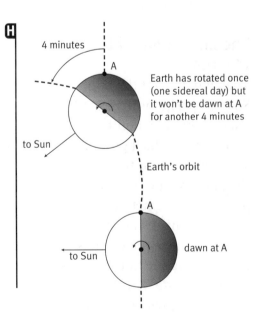

4 minutes

A

Earth has rotated once (one sidereal day) but it won't be dawn at A for another 4 minutes

to Sun

Earth's orbit

A

to Sun

dawn at A

The movement of the Moon

Like the Sun, the Moon appears to move across the sky from east to west. But unlike the Sun, it takes about an hour longer to do this.

🄷 The Moon reappears in the same part of the sky every 24 hours 49 minutes.

This longer time is explained like this:

▶ In addition to the Earth's rotation giving us a different view of the Moon, the Moon is also itself orbiting the Earth, once in about 28 days.

▶ The Moon orbits the Earth from west to east. So during the night the position of the Moon over 28 days appears to slip slowly back through the pattern of the stars.

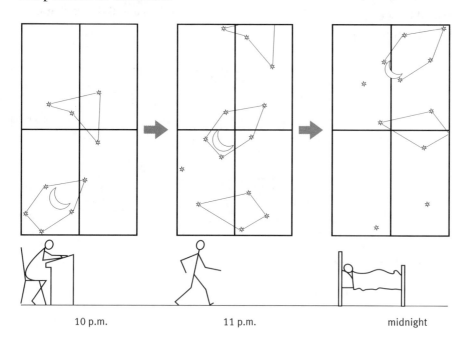

10 p.m.   11 p.m.   midnight

View through a window, showing the Moon moving east to west through the night, but slipping back relative to the pattern of stars.

🄷 The movement of the planets

The planets orbit the Sun. So their positions appear to change night by night, relative to the background of stars. For most of the time the planets move in a steady pattern, but sometimes they seem to go backwards! This is because the Earth is also orbiting the Sun, but at a different rate. The direction we see a planet depends on where both the planet and the Earth are in their orbits.

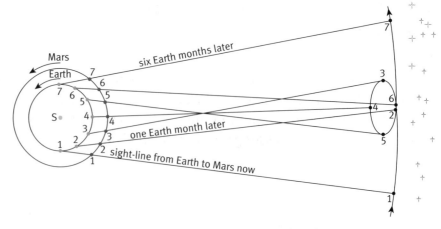

To the observer on Earth, Mars seems to be following a looped path against the fixed stars.

What causes the phases of the Moon?

We can see only the part of the Moon that is lit up by the Sun. As the Moon orbits the Earth, we see different proportions of it lit up.

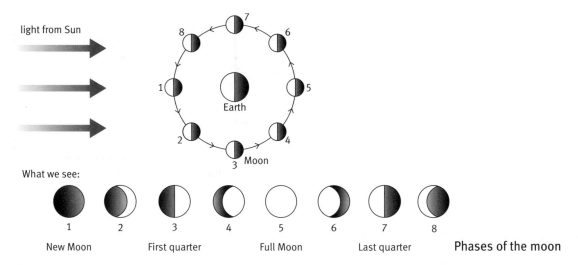

Phases of the moon

What causes an eclipse?

A **solar eclipse** is caused when light from the Sun is blocked by the Moon.

Where the Moon's full shadow falls on the Earth (the **umbra**) a total eclipse is seen. If the shadow is only partial (**penumbra**) we see a partial eclipse.

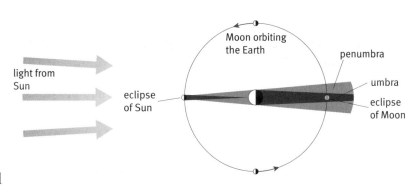

H Solar eclipses are rare because the Moon does not often line up exactly with the Sun. This is because its orbit is tilted by 5° relative to the plane of the Earth's orbit.

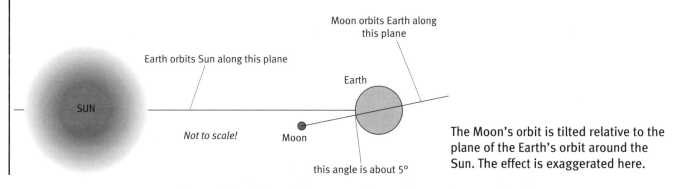

The Moon's orbit is tilted relative to the plane of the Earth's orbit around the Sun. The effect is exaggerated here.

A **lunar eclipse** is seen when the Earth's shadow blocks the sunlight from reaching the Moon. It is much more common, since the Earth's shadow is bigger than the Moon's shadow.

During a lunar eclipse the Moon can still be seen, but it looks red. This is because red light from the Sun is refracted by the Earth's atmosphere, so it can still reach the Moon's surface.

1 Charlotte has been observing the December night sky. She noticed a particular group of stars that made a pattern – her star book called this pattern 'Orion'.

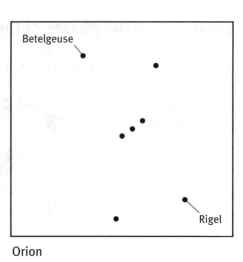

Orion

a What word is used to describe a pattern of stars like Orion?

_____ [1]

b Charlotte measures some angles and makes a careful note of the position of Orion.

How many angles does she need to identify the position of a star?

_____ angles [1]

c Charlotte looks in the same position two hours later and finds that Orion has moved. Explain why this is.

_____

_____

_____ [1]

d One star, not in Orion, does not appear to have moved. Explain why it is in the same position.

_____

_____

_____ [1]

e Charlotte looks again for Orion in June, but can't find it. Explain why this is.

_____

_____

_____ [2]

f Charlotte also notes the time at which the Moon rises for several days. Here are her results.

Date	Time of moonrise
December 24th	16:04
December 25th	17:30
December 26th	18:56
December 27th	20:20

Explain why the moonrise is getting later every day.

_____

_____

_____ [1]

g On December 24th the Moon is a full moon.

Draw what this looks like to Charlotte.

[1]

h Draw what the Moon looks like on December 27th.

Explain the difference.

_____

_____

_____ [2]

Total [10]

2 This photograph was taken in Turkey during the total eclipse of the Sun in 2006.

a Explain what causes a total eclipse.

_____

_____

_____

_____

© J Birks 2006

[1]

b Total eclipses are very rare. Use the diagram below to explain why this is.

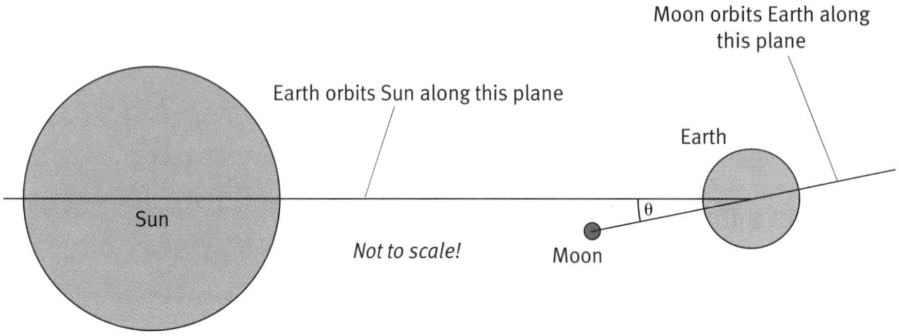

Moon orbits Earth along this plane

Earth orbits Sun along this plane

Earth

Sun

Not to scale!

Moon

θ

_____

_____

_____

[2]

c Look at the diagram above. What is the value of the angle represented as θ? (The diagram is not to scale.)

Draw a (ring) round the correct answer.

5°   **23$\frac{1}{2}$°**   **45°**

[1]

d What is the phase of the Moon during a solar eclipse?

Draw a (ring) round the correct answer.

full moon   **first quarter**   **last quarter**

new moon   **could be any phase**

[1]

e What causes a lunar eclipse?

_____

_____

_____

[1]

Total [6]

3 Two students are looking at a bright object in the night sky.

▶ Chloe says that it is a star.

▶ Kai-Wei says that, although it looks like the other stars, it is actually a planet.

a What observation(s) might the students make with the naked eye to help them decide who is right? Explain your answer.

One mark will be given for a clear, ordered argument.

_____

_____

_____

_____ [4]

b What is the difference between a star and a planet?

_____

_____ [2]

Total [6]

4 This question is about the motions of the Sun, Moon, planets and stars as observed from the Earth with the naked eye.

H **a** Choose the correct time period from the box to complete each sentence below. You may use each time once, more than once, or not at all.

23 hours 56 minutes	**24 hours**	**365 ¼ days**
29 days	**31 days**	**24 hours 49 minutes**

▶ The Sun appears to travel east-west across the sky once every _____

▶ The stars appear to travel east-west across the sky once every _____

▶ The Moon appears to travel east-west across the sky once in about _____

▶ The Earth rotates once on its axis every _____ [4]

b The ancient Greeks explained the motion of the Sun, Moon, planets and stars using a model which had the Earth at its centre. The Sun, Moon, planets and stars were arranged on crystal spheres that rotated about the Earth.

▶ Give one example of a naked-eye observation that could be explained using the Greek model.

_____ [1]

▶ Give one example of a naked-eye observation that could not easily be explained using the Greek model.

_____ [1]

Total [6]

1 Draw lines to match the words with their descriptions.

magnification	The distance between the focus and the centre of a lens
resolving power	How much bigger (in angle) the image is than the object
dioptres	A lens that is thicker in the centre than the edges, causing light rays to converge
convex lens	The spreading out of a wave as it passes through a small aperture
concave lens	The change in direction of a ray of light as it passes from one material into another
refraction	A lens that is thicker at the edges than in the centre, causing light rays to diverge
reflection	How well an instrument distinguishes objects that are close together
diffraction	The bouncing back of light at the boundary between two materials
focal length	The unit for measuring the power of a lens

2 Tick the boxes that show correct ray diagrams.

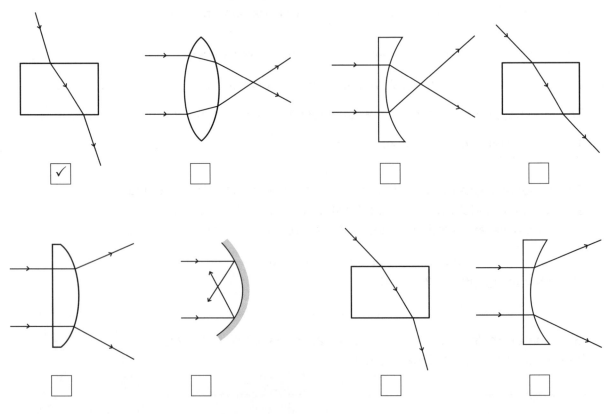

3 All these lenses are made of the same material. Arrange them in order of power – least powerful 1, most powerful 3.

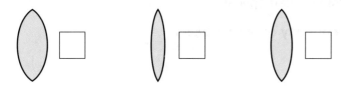

4 **a** Complete this diagram for rays going through a convex lens.

Label the position of the image.

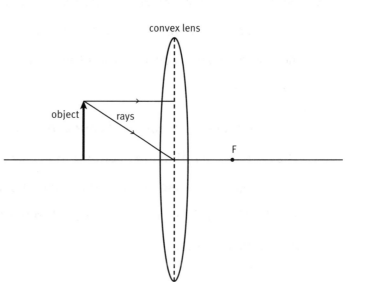

   b Draw a (ring) round the correct bold words.

The image in the diagram above is:

   ▶ **virtual / real**

   ▶ **inverted / right way up**

   ▶ **smaller / magnified**

5 Four students have measured the focal lengths of convex lenses.

   a Complete the table by calculating the power of each lens.

Student	Focal length (cm)	Power (dioptres)
Guy	50	
Kevin	20	
Nikhita	10	
Clare	40	

   b Whose lens would be the thinnest (surfaces with the least curvature)? _____

   c Which pair of lenses would make the best telescope?   _____ and _____

   d Whose lens should be used as the eyepiece lens? _____

   e How far apart should the lenses in **c** be placed? _____

   f What would be the magnification of this telescope? _____

6 Draw a ⟨ring⟩ around the correct **bold** words.

a Radio telescopes have to be **bigger / smaller** than optical telescopes because the **wavelength / frequency** of radio waves is greater than that of visible light.

b **Diffraction / reflection** reduces the **resolving power / magnification** of a telescope. This can be overcome by making the **aperture / power** much larger than the **wavelength / frequency** of the radiation being used.

c Most telescopes use **convex / concave** mirrors rather than lenses. They are called **reflecting / refracting** telescopes. One disadvantage of **lenses / mirrors** is they refract different coloured light by different amounts. It is **harder / easier** to manufacture large mirrors than lenses.

7 Write **T** next to the statements that are true.
Write **F** next to the statements that are false.

a Light from distant stars is parallel.

b The greater the focal length, the greater the power of a lens.

c Space telescopes have bigger lenses or mirrors than Earth-based telescopes.

d The atmosphere causes stars to appear to twinkle.

e Computer control enables a telescope to track a star while the Earth rotates.

f Light pollution makes it easier to see stars.

g Space telescopes can use electromagnetic waves that can't be detected at ground level.

8 Draw lines to join the beginnings of the sentences to the endings.
Draw one, two, or three lines from each beginning.

Beginnings
Disadvantages of space telescopes are that they are ...
Computers are used to control telescopes because they can ...
International cooperation in astronomy allows ...
In deciding where to site a new observatory it is necessary to consider ...

Endings
... allow the telescope to be used by an astronomer not at the observatory.
... the pooling of scientific expertise.
... the cost of new major telescopes to be shared.
... the amount of light pollution.
... enable a telescope to track a distant star while the Earth rotates.
... the environmental and social impact of the project.
... expensive to set up and maintain.
... common local weather conditions.

9 Solve the clues to fill in the grid.

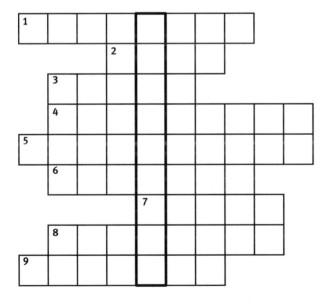

1 The light-gathering area of a telescope's objective lens.

2 A glass object used to focus light.

3 Country in which the European Southern Observatory is located.

4 The lens through which light enters a telescope.

5 Refraction by this causes stars to 'twinkle'.

6 The shape of the mirror in a reflecting telescope.

7 The path of the Hubble Space Telescope.

8 The part of a telescope you look through.

9 A British radio telescope is located at _____ Bank.

Why do we use telescopes?

Ruth is looking at the Moon with her naked eye. Shona is using a telescope to look at the Moon. The telescope has a **magnification** of 50 – it makes the Moon look 50 times larger and 50 times closer. Shona can see craters that Ruth can't see.

Now they look at the stars. The stars are so far away that they are still only points of light even through the telescope. But Shona's telescope makes the angle between the stars 50 times greater. It also collects more light, so Shona can see dimmer stars that Ruth cannot see.

What are lenses?

Shona's telescope is a **refracting** telescope. It uses lenses to form an image of a star.

Lenses are usually made from glass. Light entering the glass slows down and so it changes direction – this is called **refraction** (see Module P6). When the light leaves the glass it speeds up again, so it changes direction again. It bends the other way.

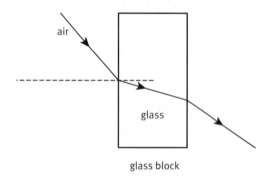

glass block

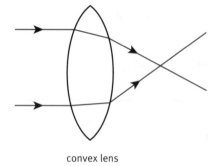

convex lens

Light rays refracting through glass

Converging and diverging lenses

A **convex** lens is thicker in the middle than at the edges.

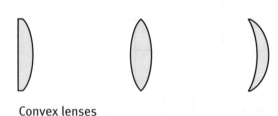

Convex lenses

Parallel rays entering a convex lens are refracted and come to a point called the **focus** – we say they **converge**.

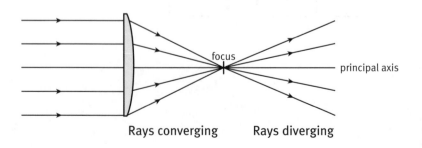

Rays converging   Rays diverging

Drawing ray diagrams

Use these rules to help you:

▶ Always use a ruler and pencil.

▶ Use arrows to show the direction that light is travelling.

▶ A ray through the centre of a lens does not change direction (ray **a**).

▶ A ray parallel to the principal axis emerges to pass through the focus (ray **b**).

▶ A ray through the focus emerges parallel to the principal axis (ray **c**).

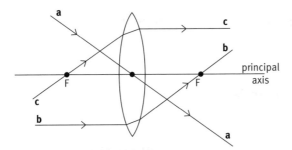

How does a convex lens form an image?

A convex lens refracts the rays of light coming from a star so that they all pass through a single point. This point is called the **image** of the star – to our eye it looks as if the star is at that point. It is called a **real image** because light rays actually come from the image. (For a 'virtual' image, like one you see in a mirror, the rays only *seem* to come from that point.)

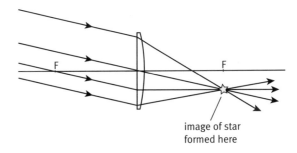

image of star formed here

Measuring the focal length

Rajul is holding a convex lens in front of the classroom wall. He moves it back and forwards until he sees a clear image of the view through the window on the wall. The distance of the lens from the wall is the **focal length** of the lens.

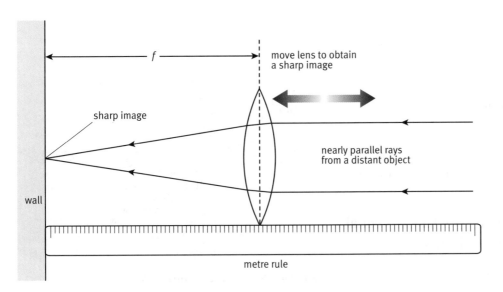

Which lens is the most powerful?

A fat convex lens, with surfaces that are more curved, has a shorter focal length than a thin lens made of the same material. The fat lens refracts the light more, and we say it is more powerful.

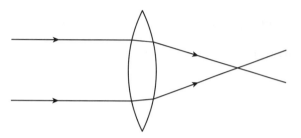
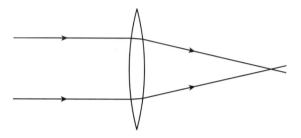

The **power** of a lens is measured in **dioptres**. You can calculate the power using the equation:

$$\text{power (in dioptres)} = \frac{1}{\text{focal length (in metres)}}$$

Why is the image upside down?

Rays from the top of the object go to the bottom of the image. So the image is **inverted**.

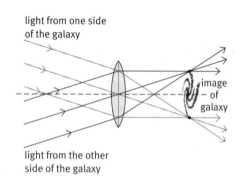

light from one side of the galaxy

image of galaxy

light from the other side of the galaxy

Building a telescope

Matthew has built a telescope using two convex lenses.

▶ The objective lens has a long focal length (low power) so that it produces a large image inside the telescope.

▶ The eyepiece lens has a short focal length (high power) and is used to magnify the real image.

▶ The distance between the two lenses is equal to the sum of the two focal lengths.

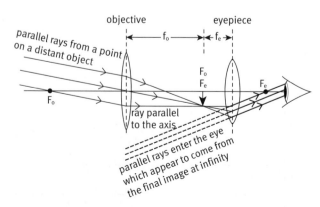

objective   eyepiece

parallel rays from a point on a distant object

ray parallel to the axis

parallel rays enter the eye which appear to come from the final image at infinity

Ray diagram for a refracting telescope

🄷 Magnification

Matthew's telescope makes the angle between stars much larger than if you looked with the naked eye. This is called the angular **magnification**. He calculates the magnification using the equation:

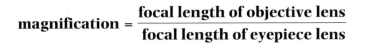

$$\text{magnification} = \frac{\text{focal length of objective lens}}{\text{focal length of eyepiece lens}}$$

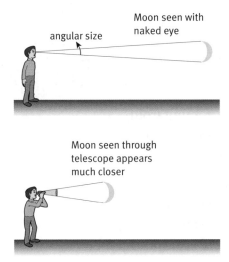

angular size

Moon seen with naked eye

Moon seen through telescope appears much closer

A telescope increases the angular size of the Moon.

Reflecting telescopes

Most telescopes actually use a concave mirror rather than a lens as the objective. A concave mirror will bring parallel light (such as that from stars) to a focus.

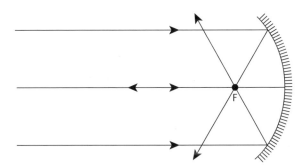

F

Reflection by a concave mirror

An eyepiece lens is then used to magnify the image from the mirror.

A reflecting telescope has advantages:

▶ It reflects all colours the same, whereas a lens will refract blue light more than red (this is called 'chromatic aberration').

▶ It is easier to make a large mirror than a large lens because its shape can be supported from the back.

▶ It is hard to make sure the glass in a lens has no imperfections.

The main disadvantage of a reflecting telescope is that the eyepiece or something similar has to be inside the telescope, so obscuring some of the image.

What other types of telescope are there?

Stars emit all the different types of electromagnetic radiation (see Module P6) not just visible light.

Radio telescopes collect radio waves coming from stars using huge parabolic reflecting dishes.

Telescopes in space can form images using other electromagnetic radiations from stars, such as X-rays and gamma rays. These radiations are absorbed by the atmosphere so can't be observed from the Earth's surface.

Why are telescopes so big?

Large telescopes are needed to collect the weak radiation coming from faint or very distant sources. The larger the **aperture** (light-gathering area of the telescope), the brighter the final image will be.

H The aperture also has to be much larger than the wavelength of the radiation being observed, otherwise **diffraction** (see Module P6) will spread the starlight out and the image will be blurred, not sharp. Radio waves have a very large wavelength, so these telescopes are enormous.

The **resolving power** of a telescope measures how well it can distinguish stars that appear close together. It depends on both the aperture size and the wavelength used.

Computers and telescopes

Paolo is an astronomer. The telescope he is using is thousands of miles away in the mountains. He uses computer controls to point the telescope towards a particular star and then track it as the Earth rotates. The image is recorded digitally and sent electronically back to his computer.

Paolo's computer can also be used to analyse or enhance images (e.g. reduce noise, improve contrast, or add false colour), and to share his observations with other scientists. Computers allow hundreds of astronomers from all over the world to share the same telescope.

Where are telescopes located?

Telescope	Location
Jodrell Bank Radio Telescope	Cheshire, UK
Arecibo Radio Telescope	Puerto Rico
Calar Alto Telescopes	Spain
European Southern Observatory	Atacama Desert, Chile

You need to learn the names and locations of at least two observatories for your exam.

Choosing a site for an optical telescope

Astronomical factors	Other factors
A mountainous (but not windy) location reduces the effects of the atmosphere, which distorts images due to refraction	Cost, including travel to and from the telescope for supplies and workers
Needs to be remote to avoid light pollution	Environmental and social impact
Good number of clear nights	Working conditions for employees

Telescopes in space

Telescopes on Earth are affected by:

▶ the atmosphere, which absorbs most infra-red, ultra-violet, X-ray and gamma radiation

▶ atmospheric refraction, which distorts images and causes stars to 'twinkle'

▶ light pollution

▶ bad weather

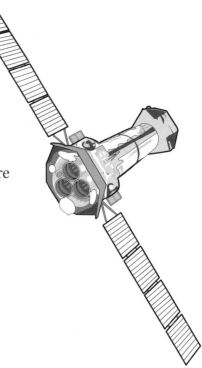

These problems can be overcome by placing the telescope in space, where there is no atmosphere, light pollution or weather. The **Hubble Space Telescope** (HST) has a resolution better than the best Earth-based telescopes.

But there are disadvantages too – mainly the high cost of setting up, maintaining, and repairing a telescope in space. There are also size limitations.

International cooperation

Collaboration between many different countries allows the cost of a major telescope to be shared and expertise pooled. For example, thirteen different countries have collaborated to run the **European Southern Observatory**, which has a number of different telescopes in Chile. Over 1000 astronomers from all over the world use this facility each year.

The XMM Newton space telescope detects X-rays from stars that can't be detected from Earth.

1 Read the following extract from a website:

> The Hubble Space Telescope (HST) was launched in 1990 as a
> joint venture between the ESA in Europe and NASA in the USA.
> The telescope has a 2.4-meter primary mirror, and its
> instrumentation allows it to work at all frequencies from infrared
> through to ultraviolet.

a Is the Hubble Space Telescope a refractor or reflector? Explain how
you know.

_____

_____   [1]

b What are the advantages of international collaboration in projects
such as HST?

_____

_____   [2]

c The Hubble Space Telescope is smaller than many Earth-based
telescopes. Why is it still able to produce higher quality images than
telescopes on Earth?

_____

_____

_____   [2]

d Give one further advantage and one disadvantage of space telescopes
as compared with Earth-based telescopes.

Advantage: _____

_____

Disadvantage: _____

_____   [2]

Total [7]

2 Astronomers used to take images of stars and galaxies using photographic film. Today it is more common for them to use 'CCDs' which use digital technology to record the image directly onto a computer, without the need for film.

a State one advantage of using CCDs for imaging compared with photographic film.

_____

_____ [1]

b As well as imaging, state and explain one further way in which computers are used in astronomy.

_____

_____

_____ [2]

Total [3]

3 Jenny is investigating how a convex lens forms an image of a distant object.

a Complete the ray diagram below showing rays from a distant, extended source passing through a convex lens. Point F is the focus of the lens.

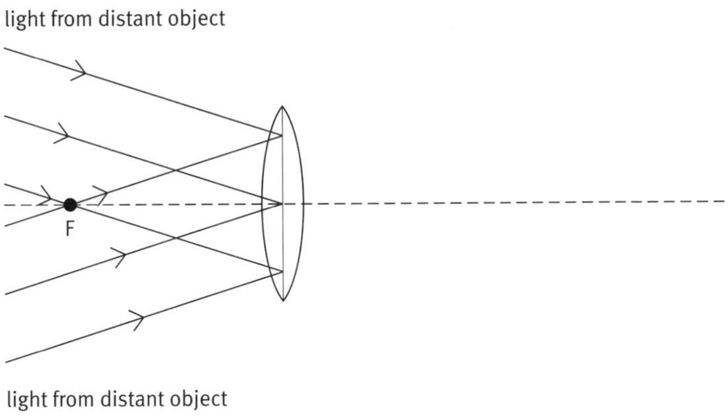

light from distant object

light from distant object

Mark the position of the image with a dotted line. [4]

b Jenny says that the image is **inverted**. Explain what this means and why it occurs. You may add to the diagram if you wish.

_____

_____

_____ [2]

Total [6]

4 This question is about a telescope.

The ray diagram below shows the arrangement of two lenses forming an astronomical telescope. The diagram is not drawn to scale.

Lens A has a focal length of 80 cm. Lens B has a focal length of 5 cm.

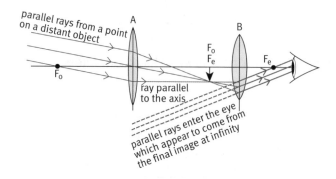

a Complete the diagram by labelling:

▶ the objective lens

▶ the principal axis

▶ the focal length of lens A   [3]

b The light rays incident on the telescope are effectively parallel.

Explain why this is.

_____

_____   [1]

c What sort of lenses are used? Tick two boxes in each column.

Lens type	Lens A	Lens B
concave		
convex		
converging		
diverging		

[1]

d Calculate the power of lens A and give the unit. Show your working.

Power of lens A = _____ _____   [2]

e How far apart should the lenses be placed in normal adjustment?

_____

_____ [1]

H

f State what is meant by angular magnification?

_____

_____ [1]

g Calculate the angular magnification of the telescope. Show your working.

Magnification = _____ [2]

h Some stars appear very dim through the telescope. How might the
telescope design be changed to improve the brightness? Tick one box.

Increase the focal length of lens A ☐

Increase the power of lens A ☐

Increase the diameter of lens A ☐

All of the above ☐ [1]

Total [12]

5   This question is about the siting of an astronomical observatory.

Read the extract below.

> **The Royal Greenwich Observatory and Telescopes**
>
> In 1675 King Charles II commissioned the building of the Royal Observatory in Greenwich, London, with the aim of providing more accurate star data for use at sea. Greenwich then was a village in open countryside, several miles from the smoke of London. The observatory's location in a Royal Park meant that no land had to be purchased, and the foundations of the previous Greenwich Castle could be used.
>
> Since then a number of different telescopes were built in Greenwich, and important observations made. However by the end of the Second World War light pollution from expanding London meant that the site was no longer as useful, and the Royal Greenwich Observatory was relocated to Herstmonceux in Sussex.
>
> A number of new telescopes were built in Sussex, including the 2.5 m Isaac Newton telescope (INT). The British climate meant that this site was never ideal, however, and in 1984 the INT was eventually moved to a high altitude, clear sky site in La Palma in the Canary Islands.

a   Underline a phrase in the first paragraph that gives an **astronomical reason** for the location of the observatory.   [1]

b   Draw a ring round a phrase in the first paragraph that gives a **non-astronomical reason** for the location of the observatory.   [1]

c   In the second paragraph, what is meant by **light pollution**?

_____

_____   [1]

d   Explain why the British climate might have been a problem for astronomy (third paragraph).

_____

_____   [1]

e   Give two advantages of having a **high altitude** site like that at La Palma.

_____

_____

_____   [2]

f   The INT is an optical telescope, collecting visible light from stars. At 2.5 m diameter it is still one of the largest in the world. Radio telescopes, however, are very much larger. Explain why radio telescopes have to be so large.

_____

_____

_____   [2]

Total [8]

1 Use these words to fill in the gaps.

charged	core	electrons	energy	fusion	ionization	join
neutrons	nucleus	pressure	protons	small	energy	temperature

_____ are negatively _____ particles on the outside of an atom.

The _____ of an atom contains positively charged _____ and

neutral _____. The _____ needed to remove an electron is

called the _____ energy. _____ is the name of the process

by which _____ nuclei can _____ together to make a larger

nucleus. This releases lots of _____. It can only happen at very high

_____ and _____, such as in the _____ of a star.

2 Use these words to label the diagram of the Geiger-Marsden experiment.

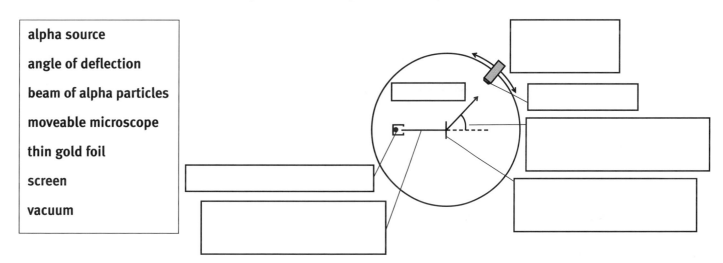

alpha source

angle of deflection

beam of alpha particles

moveable microscope

thin gold foil

screen

vacuum

3 Draw lines to match each experimental observation with the scientific explanation it supports.

Observation
Most alpha particles pass through gold foil undeflected.
The gas in a street lamp only emits light of a few frequencies (line spectra).
A few alpha particles were deflected through large angles by the gold foil.
Gases can be compressed easily.

Explanation
Atoms have a very small, dense, positive nucleus.
Electrons can have only certain energy values.
There are large empty spaces between the particles.
An atom is mostly empty space.

4 Tick the graph(s) which show(s) the correct relationship between the pressure and volume of gas at constant temperature.

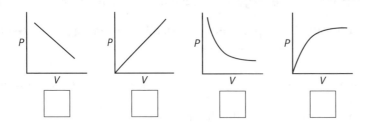

☐   ☐   ☐   ☐

5 Tick the graph(s) which show the correct relationship between the pressure and temperature of a constant volume of gas.

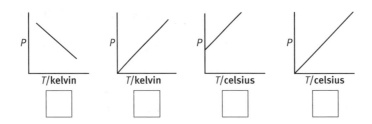

☐   ☐   ☐   ☐

6 The diagram shows the internal structure of a main sequence star. Each of the regions is described below.

Write the correct letter in each box. You may need to use some letters twice!

convective zone ☐

where fusion of hydrogen takes place ☐

where energy radiates into space ☐

photosphere ☐

core ☐

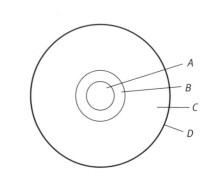

7 Place these phrases in the correct order to explain what causes the black lines in the spectrum of a star.

A A star emits photons of light with different energies.   1

B …black lines in the frequency spectrum. ☐

C These photons never reach the earth, so we observe… ☐

D …absorbed by the star's atmosphere. ☐

E The light passes through the atmosphere of the star. ☐

F Photons with certain energies are… ☐

8 This flow chart shows how stars are thought to be formed and change.
Fill in the blanks.

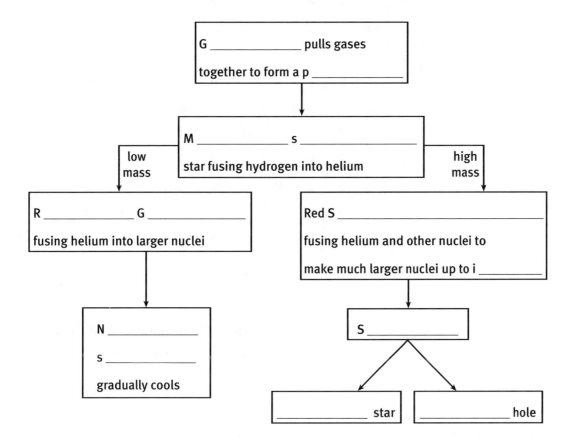

G _____ pulls gases

together to form a p _____

M _____ s _____

star fusing hydrogen into helium

low mass

high mass

R _____ G _____

fusing helium into larger nuclei

Red S _____

fusing helium and other nuclei to

make much larger nuclei up to i _____

N _____

s _____

gradually cools

S _____

_____ star   _____ hole

9 Look at the graphs showing the frequency spectra of three stars.

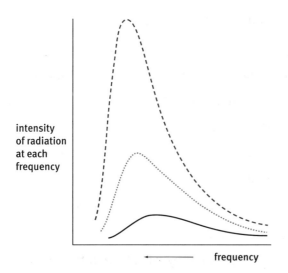

intensity
of radiation
at each
frequency

frequency

a Label the hottest star and the coolest star.

b The stars are observed to be different colours: red, white, and
yellow. Label each spectrum with the colour of the star.

10 Solve the clues, then find the answers in the wordsearch.

E	N	O	Z	E	V	I	T	C	E	V	N	O	C
R	O	E	N	E	R	G	Y	T	H	G	I	L	O
E	I	M	O	T	A	F	R	A	W	D	V	Y	R
H	S	P	A	R	T	I	C	L	E	S	L	T	E
P	U	P	R	E	S	S	U	R	E	Y	E	I	L
S	F	H	W	H	O	G	I	A	N	T	K	V	E
O	R	E	Z	E	T	U	L	O	S	B	A	A	C
T	A	L	A	V	O	N	R	E	P	U	S	R	T
O	T	O	S	T	R	O	N	G	D	L	O	G	R
H	S	H	S	U	P	E	R	G	I	A	N	T	O
P	R	O	T	O	N	S	S	U	E	L	C	U	N

a Positive particles in the nucleus of an atom. (7) _____

b The lowest theoretical temperature. (10,4) _____ _____

c The force which attracts all masses to each other. (7) _____

d The initial stage of a star. (9) _____

e Protons are held together in the nucleus by the _____ force. (6)

f A very massive star may ultimately become a black _____. (4)

g When nuclei join together. (6) _____

h The hot centre of a star. (4) _____

i The explosion at the end of the life of a red supergiant. (9) _____

j The outer radiative layer of a star. (11) _____

k In the Geiger-Marsden experiment, alpha particles were directed at _____ foil. (4)

l A negative subatomic particle. (8) _____

m Water freezes at two hundred and seventy three _____. (6)

n The central part of an atom. (7) _____

o The region of a star in which energy is transferred by convection. (10, 4) _____ _____

p When hydrogen fusion stops, our Sun will become a red _____. (5)

q When hydrogen fusion stops, a very massive star would become a red _____. (10)

r Our Sun is a main sequence _____. (4)

s If you decrease the volume of a gas at constant temperature, its _____ increases. (8)

t Produced during fusion and radiated from a star. (6) _____

u The smallest piece of any element. (4) _____

v The radiation by which we can see a star. (5) _____

w When a red giant stops fusion, it shrinks to become a white _____. (5)

x In a gas there are large spaces between the _____. (9)

What is an atom like?

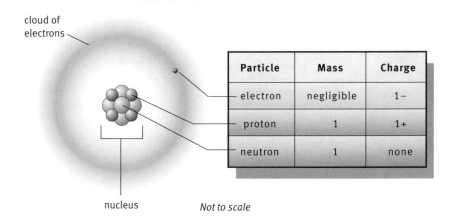

Particle	Mass	Charge
electron	negligible	1–
proton	1	1+
neutron	1	none

Not to scale

The nucleus is only about $1/100\,000$ (or one hundred-thousandth) of the diameter of an atom.

The protons are all positively charged. Positive charges repel (**electrostatic repulsion**) but they are held together by another force called the **strong nuclear force**.

Evidence for the nuclear atom

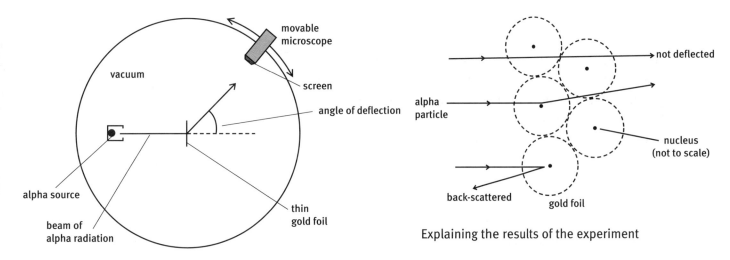

The Rutherford–Geiger–Marsden experiment of 1909

Explaining the results of the experiment

Most alpha particles passed straight through the foil without any deflection, showing that atoms are mostly empty space.

A very tiny fraction of alpha particles were 'back-scattered' through angles greater than 90°. They must have come close to a very tiny, very heavy, positively charged nucleus. This experiment led to the model of the atom with a central, positive nucleus.

Nuclear fusion

Stars like our Sun are mostly made of hydrogen. In the centre of a star it is so hot that the atoms lose all of their electrons. When hydrogen nuclei come very close together the nuclei **fuse** (join together) to make helium. Nuclear fusion releases vast amounts of energy, which stars emit as electromagnetic radiation (see Modules P2 and P6).

The structure of stars

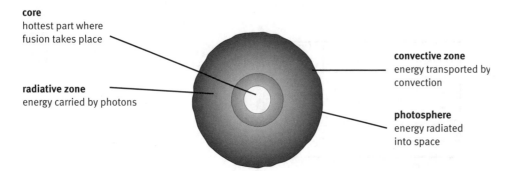

core
hottest part where
fusion takes place

radiative zone
energy carried by photons

convective zone
energy transported by
convection

photosphere
energy radiated
into space

Section through a main squence star

Spectra and temperature

Stars radiate energy across all wavelengths of the electromagnetic spectrum. But different stars emit different amounts of radiation at different frequencies, depending on their temperature – this is why the coolest stars appear **red**, slightly hotter ones **orange**, then **yellow**, **white**, and the hottest stars appear **blue-white**.

Astronomers can use a **spectrometer** to measure how much radiation is emitted at each frequency, and get an accurate value for the temperature of the star from the **peak frequency**. The greater the peak frequency, the higher the temperature.

The shape of the frequency spectrum is the same for all stars, and for all hot objects.

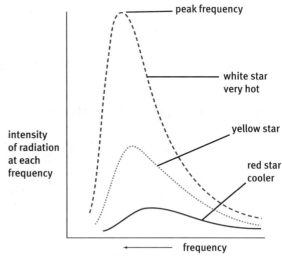

peak frequency

white star
very hot

yellow star

red star
cooler

intensity
of radiation
at each
frequency

frequency

Frequency spectra of
different stars

Scientists can also work out the size of a star from its temperature and the total amount of radiation it produces a second (called its **luminosity**). This is given by the area under each line in the graph above.

The Hertzsprung–Russell diagram

This is a plot of the luminosity (intrinsic brightness) of a star against its colour or temperature. Note that the temperature axis goes from hot to cold!

Stars like our Sun, which fuse hydrogen to make helium, are called **main sequence** stars. There is a clear correlation between temperature and intrinsic brightness – the hotter a main sequence star, the more radiation it emits.

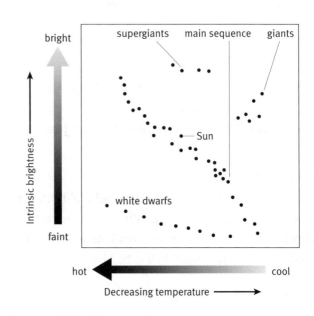

bright

supergiants   main sequence   giants

Intrinsic brightness

Sun

white dwarfs

faint

hot   cool

Decreasing temperature

Red giants are stars that are past their hydrogen fusing stage and are fusing helium and heavier elements. The colour red means they are cool, but they are still very bright because of their huge sizes.

White dwarfs are very hot stars, but they are not very bright due to their very small size.

Absorption lines

Electrons in an atom can have only certain energy values. They can move between energy levels only if they are given exactly the right amount of energy. (With enough energy they can leave the atom completely and this is called **ionization**.)

When light emitted from a star passes through the star's atmosphere some of the photons (packets of energy) have exactly the right amount of energy (that is, the right frequency) to move electrons to higher energy levels. The atmosphere therefore **absorbs** these frequencies and no light of those frequencies reaches the Earth – we observe black lines in the spectrum of light.

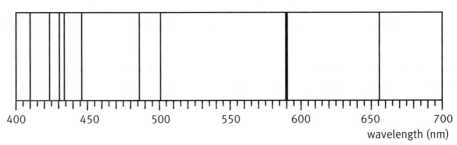

Every type of atom has its own unique electron energies, producing its own unique pattern of 'missing lines' in an absorption spectrum. Scientists can readily identify which elements make up a star by comparing the lines in the absorption spectrum with the emission spectra of elements in the laboratory. Stars like our Sun are mostly made from hydrogen and helium.

The spectrum of visible light from a star, showing black absorption lines

What are gases like?

Stars are giant balls of hot gases. To understand stars, you need to understand gases.

The particles of a gas (atoms or molecules) move very quickly in random directions. When they hit the sides of a container they exert a force as they change direction. This is what causes gas **pressure**.

Particle model of a gas

Pressure and volume

If you decrease the volume of the container, the particles will hit the sides more often and so the pressure will go up.

Volume and pressure are said to be **inversely proportional**. Doubling volume will halve the pressure, and halving the volume will double the pressure (if the temperature is kept the same).

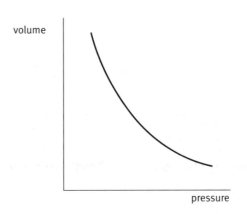

Increasing the pressure on a gas reduces its volume (at constant temperature).

Temperature and pressure

Temperature corresponds to the energy of the gas particles. The hotter the gas, the faster the particles move, and the harder and more often they will hit the sides of the container.

So increasing the temperature will increase the pressure of a gas. And decreasing the temperature will decrease the pressure of the gas.

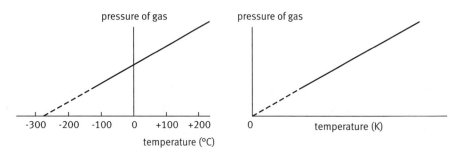

Increasing the temperature of a gas increases its pressure (at constant volume).

If you continue to cool a gas the particles will move slower and slower. At the lowest imaginable temperature the particles would no longer be moving at all and so would never hit the sides of the container! This theoretical temperature is called **absolute zero** and corresponds to **−273 °C**.

Scientists sometimes use a temperature scale that starts at absolute zero, called the **Kelvin scale**. The divisions are called **kelvin (K)** rather than degrees Celsius.

Temperature in K = temperature in °C + 273

Temperature in °C = temperature in K − 273

Temperature and volume

If you decrease the temperature of a gas at fixed pressure, the volume of the gas will also decrease. At a temperature of absolute zero, the volume would theoretically be zero!

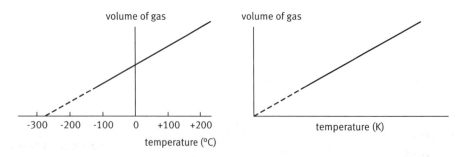

Increasing the temperature of a gas increases its volume (at constant pressure).

How are stars formed?

Stars are formed when gravity compresses a cloud of gas. The volume goes down and both the pressure and temperature go up.

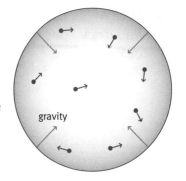

As the particles fall towards each other they go faster and faster and so the temperature of the gas rises. Eventually the temperature and pressure become so high that **fusion** starts and a star is formed. The early stage of a star, when it is still being compressed under the force of gravity, is called a **protostar**.

Eventually the collision pressures resulting from fusion (called **radiation pressure**) balance the force of gravity and the star becomes stable. It is then known as a **main sequence star**.

The life cycle of a star

Throughout its life as a main sequence star, hydrogen is being fused to form helium. Eventually the hydrogen in the core will run out. The core of the star collapses inwards where new fusion reactions begin, causing the outer layers to expand, and forming a **red giant**. Very large stars become **red supergiants**.

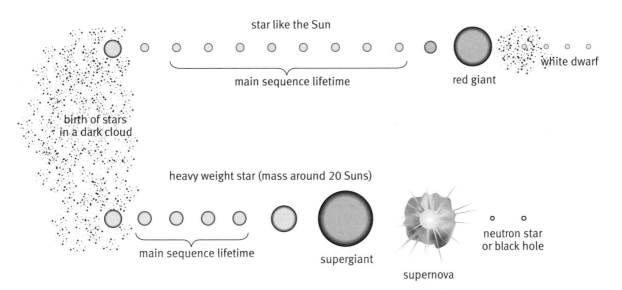

The core of a red giant becomes hot enough for helium nuclei to start fusing together. This makes heavier elements such as carbon, nitrogen, and oxygen. Inside a red supergiant the core pressure is much higher still, and all of the elements up to iron may be formed by fusion reactions.

Eventually all fusion will cease. The core remaining from a red giant will become a **white dwarf**, which will slowly cool and become less bright.

Red supergiants however undergo a huge explosion called a **supernova** – clouds of dust and gas are blown outwards. These may eventually form new protostars as the cycle begins again. The remaining very dense cores become either **neutron stars** or **black holes**.

1 Look at the diagram showing the frequency spectra of three different stars.

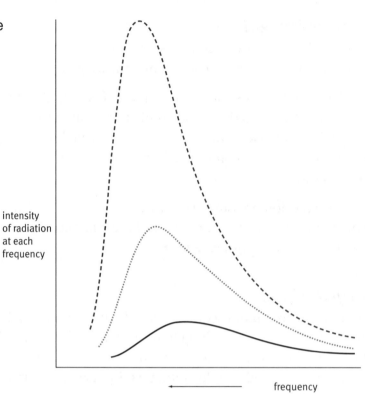

intensity of radiation at each frequency

frequency

a What does the peak frequency tell an astronomer about a star?

_____ [1]

b What does the area under each curve represent?

_____ [1]

c Label which of the three stars is the hottest. [1]

d The diagram shows that the stars produce a continuous range of radiation right across the electromagnetic spectrum. Explain why not all of this radiation can be detected on Earth.

_____

_____ [1]

e A close analysis of the spectrum shows there are black lines due to certain missing frequencies.

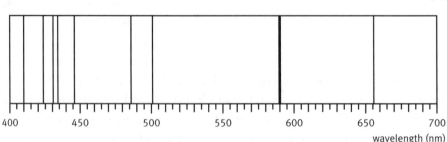

400   450   500   550   600   650   700
wavelength (nm)

What can an astronomer learn from these missing frequencies?

_____ [1]

f Explain, in terms of your knowledge of atomic structure, what causes the black lines.

_____

_____ [1]

Total [6]

2 This question is about gases.

    a A gas cylinder contains hydrogen gas at high pressure. Explain, in terms of the particles making up the gas, what causes its pressure. You may be awarded a mark for the clarity of your answer.

    _____

    _____

    _____ [3]

    b On a hot day the gas in the cylinder gets very warm. Describe, in terms of particles, the difference between a hot gas and a cooler gas.

    _____ [1]

    c Explain the process by which pressure increases as a cool gas gets hotter.

    Explain your answer, in terms of the particles.

    _____

    _____

    _____ [2]

    Total [6]

3 In 1909 Geiger and Marsden carried out a famous experiment. They bombarded a very thin piece of gold foil with alpha particles.

    a What feature of their results led to the conclusion that atoms have a very dense, positive nucleus?

    _____

    _____ [1]

    b What feature of their results led to the conclusion that the atom was mostly empty space?

    _____

    _____ [1]

    c What two sorts of particles are now known to make up the nucleus of an atom?

    _____ [2]

    d Protons in the nucleus repel each other. Why doesn't the nucleus fall apart?

    _____

    _____ [1]

    Total [5]

4 This question is about stars.

Nissa is an astronomer. She has been using a space telescope to find out about a group of four stars. A spectrometer on the telescope was used to split the light from each star into its different frequencies.

a How will Nissa determine the surface temperature of each star?

_____

_____ [1]

b What feature of a star's spectrum will allow her to determine what elements are present in each star?

_____

_____ [1]

c Most scientists think that the early Universe consisted mainly of hydrogen gas. Explain how a star might be formed from this hydrogen gas.

_____

_____

_____

_____ [3]

The table below lists the stars that Nissa has data for.

Star letter	Mass compared to Sun	Type of star	Colour	Heavy elements present?
A	1.9	main sequence	yellow	yes
B	90	main sequence	white	yes
C	0.4	main sequence	orange	no
D	4.5	red giant	red	yes

d What process is happening in the core of a main sequence star?

_____ [1]

e Write a word equation for this process.

_____

_____ [2]

f How is the process in the core of a red giant different from that for a main sequence star?

_____

_____ [2]

g Some main sequence stars contain heavy elements such as iron, some do not. What does the presence of heavy elements in a main sequence star tell Nissa about the likely history of that star?

_____

_____ [1]

h At the end of its life as a red giant, what type of star might star D become?

Draw a (ring) round the correct answer.

supernova   **protostar**   **white dwarf**

red dwarf   **red supergiant**
[1]

i What determines when this change will happen?

_____

_____ [1]

j Which of the main sequence stars is most likely to become a supernova eventually? Give a reason for your choice.

_____

_____ [1]

k Following the supernova explosion, what are two possible outcomes for the star?

_____

_____ [2]

Total [16]

5 The diagram shows the internal structure of a main sequence star.

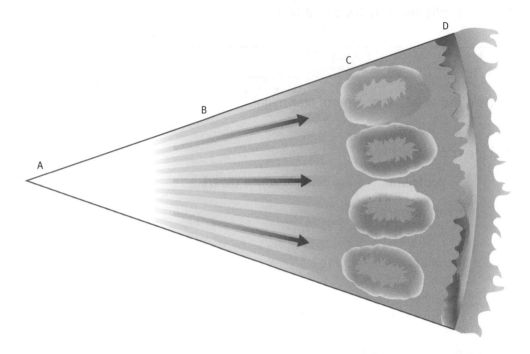

a What name is given to the part of the star labelled D?

_____   [1]

b How is energy transported through the part of the star labelled C?

_____   [1]

c A particular star has a surface temperature of 5500 K.

What is this in degrees Celsius? _____   [1]

d The core has a much higher temperature than this. Explain, in terms
of the particle model, why a very high temperature and a very high
pressure are needed for fusion to take place.

Temperature _____

_____

Pressure _____

_____   [2]

e The enormous amounts of energy produced by fusion gives rise to
an outward force on the material of the star, called radiation pressure.
Why doesn't the star explode outwards?

_____   [1]

f Our Sun is a main sequence star. It is thought that eventually it will change, becoming a red giant.

   i What will cause this change to take place?

   _____   [1]

   ii What determines whether a star becomes a red giant or a red supergiant?

   _____   [1]

g Whilst stars are very hot, most of space is very cold, with a temperature of about 3 kelvin. What is this temperature in degrees Celsius?

   _____   [1]

h Use the particle model of a gas to explain why it is not possible for a gas to be cooler that zero kelvin.

   _____

   _____

   _____   [1]

Total [10]

1 Draw lines to match the words and descriptions.

parallax	A group of thousands of millions of stars
parsec	How closer stars seem to move over time relative to more distant ones
light-year	A star whose brightness varies periodically
nebula	The distance that light travels in one year
galaxy	The distance to a star with a parallax angle of one second of arc
Cepheid variable	Name once given to any fuzzy object seen in the night sky

2 Look at the data in the table.

Star	Parallax angle (seconds of arc)	Colour
A	0.52	yellow
B	0.015	orange
C	0.084	white
D	0.17	blue-white

a Which star is the closest?

b Which star is the furthest away?

c Which star is the hottest?

d Which star is the coolest?

3 Draw a (ring) round the correct bold words.

a The **parallax angle / temperature** of a star is related to its distance away.

b The period of a **Cepheid variable / supernova** is related to its brightness.

c The **speed / period** at which a galaxy is moving away is related to its **distance / temperature**.

d The **luminosity / speed of recession** of a star depends on its temperature and size.

e The observed brightness of a star depends on its **luminosity / Hubble constant** and its **distance away / period**.

4 In the 1920s there was a great debate between the astronomers Curtis and Shapley. Edwin Hubble later provided evidence that proved one of them to be correct.

Complete the speech bubbles.

Curtis

> I think the nebulae are distant galaxies, outside of our galaxy.

Shapley

> You're wrong. I think they are… _____
>
> _____

Hubble

> I have used a Cepheid variable star to… _____
>
> _____

> My measurements show that… _____
>
> _____
>
> So _____ must be right.

5 The graph shows data published by Hubble in 1929.

Use these words to complete the graph labels and fill in the gaps below.

accurately	away	distance of galaxy from Earth	distance	graph
Hubble	light	measure	period	redshift	speed
speed of recession	uncertain	Universe	variable	galaxy

Hubble used the _____ of Cepheid

_____ stars to measure the

_____ to galaxies. The _____

from these galaxies is redshifted. This means that

they are moving _____, and the

_____ is expanding. The speed of

recession can be found from the amount of

_____.

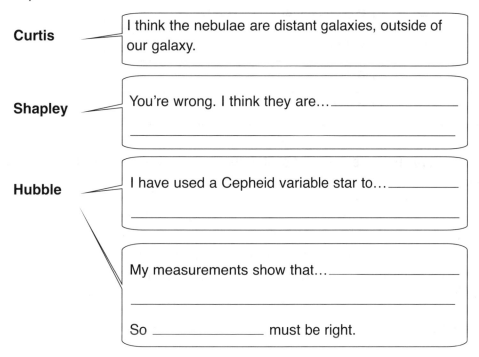

(km/s)

(light-years)

Hubble found that as the distance to a _____ increases, the _____ of

recession increases. The gradient of the _____ is called the _____

constant. Its exact value is _____ as it is difficult to _____ the distances

_____.

6 a Complete the table.

Star	Parallax angle (seconds of arc)	Distance (parsecs)
Kapteyn's Star	0.250	
Procyon	0.285	
Sirius	0.370	

b Why can't parallax be used to find stellar distances greater than 100 parsecs?

_____

c Alpha-Centauri, the next nearest star after the sun, is 1.2 parsecs away from Earth. Which of the following gives its distance in light-years?

4.3 light-years ☐

43 light-years ☐

4300 light-years ☐

4.3 light-seconds ☐

d The Hubble Law is given by the equation:

speed of recession (km/s) = **Hubble constant** (s⁻¹) × **distance** (km)

Assuming the Hubble constant to be 2×10^{-18} s⁻¹, calculate the recessional speed of a galaxy 3×10^{21} km away.

_____

_____

e Another galaxy has a recessional speed of 2000 km/s. How far away is it?

_____

_____

f The distance to a Cepheid variable is measured as 4.3×10^{20} km, and its recessional speed as 990 km/s. What value does this give for the Hubble constant?

_____

_____

7 Write **T** next to the statements that are true.

Write **F** next to the statements that are false.

a A smaller parallax angle means that a star is closer to us.

b A parsec is similar in magnitude to a light-year.

c A megaparsec is a million parsecs.

d Typical interstellar distances are measured in megaparsecs.

e Cepheid variable stars pulse in brightness.

f Cepheid variables with a longer period have a greater luminosity.

g The Sun is a star in the Milky Way galaxy.

h Typical intergalactic distances are measured in megaparsecs.

i The further away a star is, the lower its luminosity.

8 Put these sentences in the correct order to show how an astronomer can work out distance from a Cepheid variable star.

A Plot the observed brightness of the Cepheid variable over several months.

B Compare the observed brightness with the luminosity to find the distance.

C Use the period to work out its luminosity.

D Find the period of the Cepheid variable from the graph.

9 Solve the clues to complete the grid and reveal the name of a famous scientist.

What is she famous for?

1 Our galaxy (5-3)

2 Seen through a telescope, this appears as a fuzzy patch of light (6)

3 Scientist who debated with Curtis about whether there were galaxies outside of our own (7)

4 A star that pulses in brightness (7, 8)

5 Distance light travels in a year (5–4)

6 Can be determined from the peak frequency of the radiation emitted by a star (11)

7 Data from an absorption spectrum, used to calculate the recession speed of distant galaxies (8)

Light-years

A light-year is the **distance** light travels in one year. After the Sun, the nearest stars are about four light-years away – this means that we see the light that left those stars four years ago. Some galaxies are thought to be millions of light-years away – looking at them is looking back in time!

Using parallax

As the Earth orbits the Sun, the closest stars appear to change their positions relative to the very distant 'fixed stars' – this effect is called **parallax**. The stars haven't actually moved – the Earth, from which we are observing, from has moved.

The **parallax angle** is half the angle apparently moved in six months (when the Earth has travelled from one side of the Sun to the other).

▶ Parallax angles are very small – measured in **seconds of arc**. (1 degree of arc = 60 minutes, 1 minute of arc = 60 seconds)

▶ The smaller the parallax angle, the further the star is away:

$$\text{distance to star (in parsecs)} = \frac{1}{\text{parallax angle (in seconds of arc)}}$$

A **parsec (pc)** is the distance to a star whose parallax angle is one second of arc. It is about the same as 3 light-years.

▶ The distance between stars within a galaxy is usually a few parsecs.
▶ Distances between galaxies are measured in **megaparsecs (Mpc)**. (1 Mpc = 1 000 000 pc)

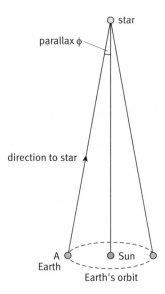

Defining the parallax angle

Why are some stars brighter than others?

The **luminosity** (intrinsic brightness) of a star describes the total amount of radiation it emits every second. It depends on the star's **temperature** and **surface area** – the hotter and larger the star, the more energy radiated per second.

▶ **Red giants** are bright because they are very large, even though they are relatively cool.
▶ **White dwarfs** are quite dim, even though they are extremely hot, because they are very small.

The **observed brightness** we see from Earth depends not only on a star's luminosity but also on its distance. The further away a star is, the dimmer it seems to be. This is because the light has been spread out over a bigger area.

Scientists can calculate the distance to a star knowing its observed brightness and its luminosity.

Hussein's torch seems dimmer than Sean's identical torch, because he is further away.

Cepheid variables

Cepheid variables are a type of star whose brightness varies in a regular way over a period of a few days (due to changes in the star's size). The time between peaks of brightness is called the **period**.

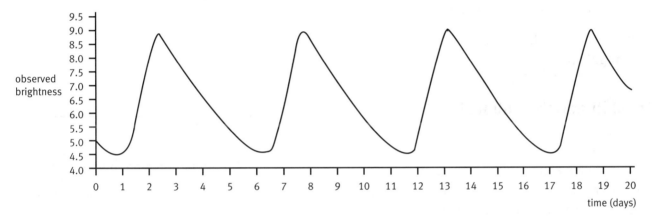

Variation in the brightness of Delta Cephei with time

Working out distances using Cepheid variables

A scientist called Henrietta Leavitt discovered that there is a correlation between the luminosity of a Cepheid variable and its period – the greater the luminosity, the longer the period.

Scientists can therefore work out the distance to all Cepheid variable stars like this:

▶ Measure the period.
▶ Use the period to work out the luminosity.
▶ Measure the observed brightness.
▶ Compare the observed brightness with the luminosity to get the distance.

Distances to many galaxies are too large to measure using parallax. Instead astronomers look for a Cepheid variable within that galaxy and use its period and brightness to find the distance.

Observing nebulae and galaxies

Telescopes show that our galaxy, the Milky Way, is made up from thousands of millions of stars. Our Sun is just one of them.

At first scientists were puzzled by some fuzzy patches of light observed by astronomers – they called them **nebulae**. There was a great debate about them in the 1920s.

▶ **Shapley** thought the Milky Way was the entire Universe and so the nebulae were clouds of gas within the Milky Way.
▶ **Curtis** thought that that they were huge, distant clusters of stars – other galaxies outside the Milky Way.
▶ Further evidence came from the astronomer **Hubble**. He found a Cepheid variable in the Andromeda Nebula, and measured its distance. It was much further away than any star in the Milky Way – it had to be a separate galaxy.

Cepheid variables have been used to show that most 'nebulae' are, in fact, distant galaxies.

Redshift and the Hubble law

When astronomers look at the absorption spectra from distant galaxies, they find that the black absorption lines are all shifted towards the red end of the spectrum – this is called **redshift**.

The speed of recession of a galaxy can be found from its redshift.

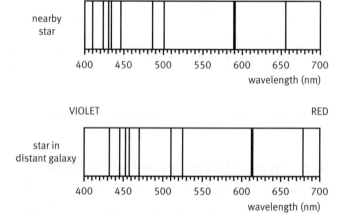

The absorption spectrum from a distant galaxy shows redshift.

By measuring the distances to these galaxies using Cepheid variable stars, Hubble found that more distant galaxies are moving away with a greater speed. He wrote this as an equation:

speed of recession = Hubble constant × distance

Hubble's results can be explained if all the galaxies are moving away from each other – in other words, the Universe is expanding.

This law gave support to **big bang** theory – that the Universe started from one tiny point, and has been expanding in size ever since.

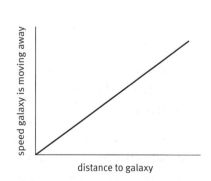

1 Look at this graph showing the variation of brightness of the star TU Cassiopeiae.

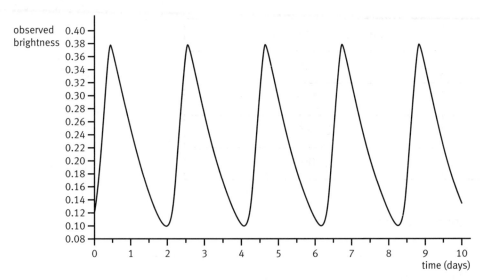

a What sort of star is TU Cassiopeiae? Draw a (ring) around the correct answer.

   neutron star   **supernova**   **Cepheid variable**   **red giant**   [1]

b Use the graph above to work out the period of the star.

   _____   [1]

c The period can be linked to the luminosity of a star.

   Use your answer to part **b** and the graph below to work out the
   luminosity of TU Cassiopeiae.

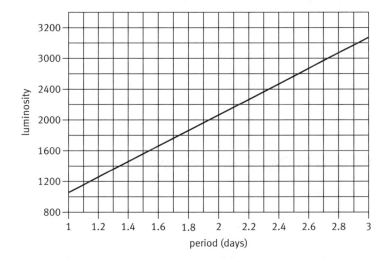

Answer: _____ units   [1]

d Using the average observed brightness and the luminosity
   of the star, what else can an astronomer find out?

   The temperature of the star   ☐

   The Hubble constant   ☐

   The distance to the star   ☐

   The size of the star   ☐   [1]

Total **[4]**

2   A data book gives parallax angles for various astronomical objects:

Name	Parallax angle/seconds of arc
Sirius A	0.38
Orion nebula	0.002
61 Cygnus	0.286
Crab nebula	0.0005

a   Explain what is meant by parallax.

_____

_____

_____   [2]

b   Without doing any calculation, which object is closest to Earth?

Explain how you know.

_____

_____   [2]

c   Calculate the distance to 61 Cygnus in parsecs. Show your working.

Distance = _____ parsecs   [2]

d   Another data book gives the distance to 61 Cygnus as 11 light-years.

What is a light-year?

_____

_____   [2]

e   An astronomer says, 'Looking at stars is looking back in time.'
    Explain what she means.

_____

_____

_____   [1]

Total [9]

3 This question is about galaxies.

a Explain what a 'galaxy' is.

_____

_____ [1]

b What is the name of our galaxy? Draw a ring around the correct answer.

Orion   Andromeda   Milky Way   Cygnus   Cassiopeia [1]

c The distance to a certain star has been measured as 230 megaparsecs.
Is the star in our galaxy or in another? Explain how you know.

_____

_____

_____ [1]

d The astronomer Edwin Hubble found evidence that distant galaxies
are all moving away from the Earth. His result can be written
as an equation:

speed of recession (km/s) = Hubble constant (s^{-1}) × distance to galaxy (km)

A galaxy estimated to be 1.5×10^{21} km away has a measured speed of
recession of 3500 km/s. Use this equation to calculate a value for the
Hubble constant. Show your working.

Hubble constant = _____ s^{-1} [2]

e Explain why it is difficult to get a precise value for the Hubble constant.

_____

_____

_____

_____ [1]

Total [6]

4 Cassiopeia is a group of stars that form a 'W' shape in the night sky. Seen from Earth the main stars all have a similar brightness.

a James says, 'The stars all look to have the same brightness, so they must all be about the same distance away.' Explain why he may not be right.

_____

_____

_____

_____ [2]

b The distance to one of the stars, called Caph, is given by a data book as 14 parsecs. What is a parsec?

_____

_____ [2]

c With a good telescope, several 'fuzzy' patches of light can also be seen in the region of Cassiopeia.

What name did astronomers once give such objects?

_____ [1]

d In 1920 a debate was held between two astronomers, Curtis and Shapley, about these objects.

Explain what was the main issue of the debate.

_____

_____

_____

_____ [2]

Total [7]

Developing explanations

1 It's 1979. Scientists Luis and Walter Alvarez are discussing an exciting find:

This 65-million-year-old rock we found. It's got iridium in it. And the iridium concentration is the same as the iridium concentration in an asteroid.

*That's interesting **data**. Let's think about it.*

2 A few days later:

*I've thought of an **explanation that accounts for our data**. An asteroid collided with Earth 65 million years ago. The collision caused a huge dust cloud that blocked out the sunlight for many years. This killed off all the dinosaurs.*

That's a pretty creative explanation! It links in well to some other data, too: no one has ever found dinosaur fossils in rocks younger than 65 million years old.

3 A few years later:

It says here that scientists have found an asteroid crater in Mexico. And we know that there is iridium in 65-million-year-old rocks all over the world. This extra data has made me even more confident in our explanation!

Why?

I agree about the first part of the explanation – an asteroid colliding with Earth. But I'm less confident about the second part; that the collision made dinosaurs extinct.

Well, there's evidence from other scientists that dinosaurs were already starting to die out before the collision. Also, there haven't been mass extinctions every time an asteroid hit Earth. Maybe it's time to think again...

4 It's 1924. Two scientists are reporting their latest fossil find.

Developing explanations

1 The statements below describe how a scientist developed an explanation about the origin of life on Earth.

Write the letter of each statement in an appropriate place on the flow chart. Some boxes need more than one letter.

A There are volcanic vents where tectonic plates meet on the sea floor. The vents spew out water, methanol, and other chemicals at about 300 °C.

B Methanol is a simple organic molecule. Normally, methanol molecules break down at 300 °C.

C The volcanic vents contain clay minerals.

D Most scientists believe that life evolved from simple organic (carbon-based) molecules.

E A scientist thought that the clay in volcanic vents might be important. Maybe it could stop methanol breaking down. Perhaps the clay could also help to make bigger organic molecules.

F The scientist thought that, eventually, the clay and organic molecules move out of the volcanic vents. They go to cooler water. Here, life may begin.

G The scientist predicted that, in the lab, clay would protect methanol and help to make bigger organic molecules.

H The scientist made a model undersea volcanic vent in her lab. She observed what happened for six weeks.

I Her prediction was correct.

J Another scientist thinks life is more likely to have started in cooler springs under the ocean. These warm springs have all the ingredients to make organic molecules.

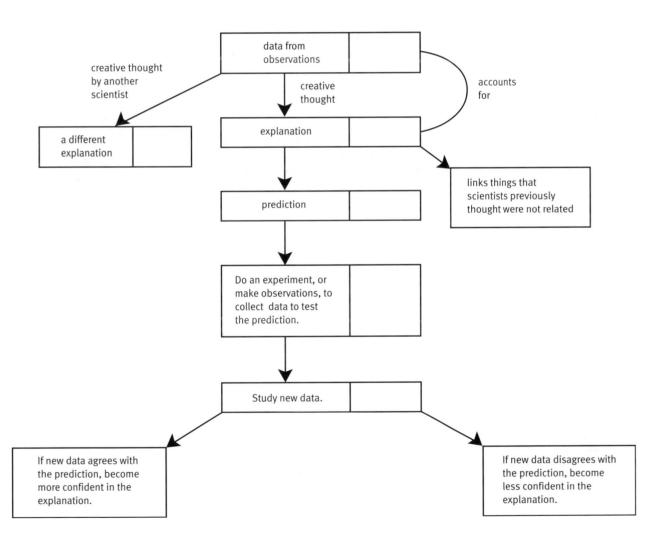

2 The statements below describe how a scientist developed an explanation about mass extinctions.

Write the letter of each statement in an appropriate place on the flow chart. Some boxes need more than one letter.

A Scientists have found 10 enormous lava sheets on the Earth's surface.

B The biggest lava sheet is in Siberia. It is 252 million years old.

C There is lava sheet in India that is 66 million years old.

D No one has found dinosaur fossils in rocks younger than 65 million years old.

E About 251 million years ago 95% of all species became extinct.

F American scientists think that meteorites slammed into the Earth 66 million years ago and 252 million years ago.

G They believe the meteorites pierced the Earth's crust. Lava and carbon dioxide gas rushed out of the holes.

H The scientists think that the extra carbon dioxide gas made the Earth so hot that many species became extinct.

I The scientists predicted that a computer model would show that meteorites had enough energy to pierce the Earth and release enough lava to make the lava sheets.

J The scientists ran the computer model.

K Their prediction was correct.

L Other scientists think that volcanoes erupted in Siberia 252 million years ago. This led to decreased amounts of oxygen in the sea, and caused a mass extinction.

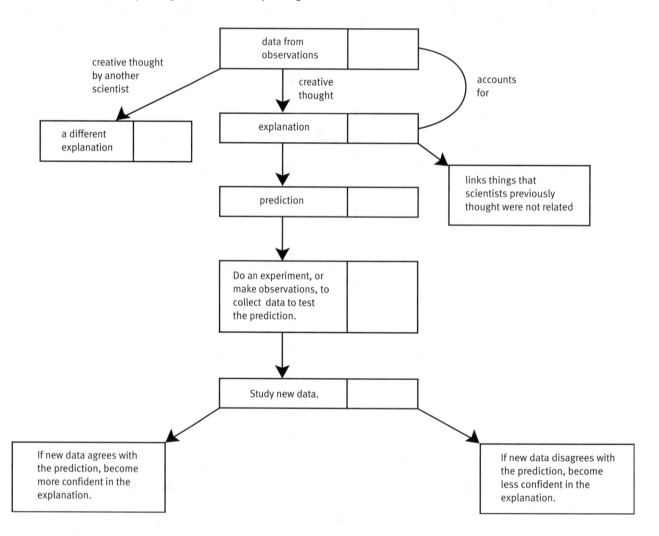

Developing explanations

1 In Kenya, elephants sometimes go onto farmland and ruin maize crops. Some farmers kill these elephants.

Scientists wanted to explain why elephants go onto farmland.
They could then predict when elephants were likely to go onto farmland.
The scientists could then tell farmers when to make the most effort
to guard their crops from elephants.

The scientists studied seven elephants.

They found out where the elephants went and what they ate.

The statements below describe the scientists' work.

A Scientists plan to work with farmers to help them protect their crops from elephants.	
B Satellite tracking showed that six elephants spent all their time in the lowlands.	
C Tail hair analysis from one elephant showed that he ate grass from the lowlands in wet seasons and maize from farmland in dry seasons.	
D In the dry season, there is not enough grass for elephants to eat. Some elephants get the food they need from shrubs and trees. But if there are not enough trees and shrubs, elephants take maize from farmland to eat.	
E Satellite tracking showed that one elephant spent the wet season in the lowlands and the dry season in a forest near farmland.	
F Tail hair analysis of six elephants showed that they ate trees and shrubs in the dry season. In the wet season they ate grass.	
G Fewer elephants will die if scientists find out when they are most likely to eat maize from farms.	

Some of these statements are **data** and one is a possible **explanation**.
Write a **D** next to the **four** statements that are data.
Write an **E** next to the **one** statement that is an explanation.

Total [5]

2 Scientists collected this data:

▶ All around the world, rocks from 65 million years ago contain high levels of iridium.

▶ Asteroids contain iridium.

From the data, they developed this **explanation**:

> An asteroid hitting the Earth 65 million years ago caused rocks of that age to contain high levels of iridium.

Other scientists used the explanation and extra data to make a prediction:

> **Extra data:** Asteroids and comets were made at the same time.
> **Prediction:** Comet tail dust contains iridium.

The scientists use a spacecraft to collect comet tail dust.
They will examine the dust to find out if it contains iridium.

Tick the boxes next to the **two** statements that are true.

If they find iridium, this will confirm the prediction. ☐

If they find iridium, this will prove the explanation is correct. ☐

If they do not find iridium, this will show that the prediction is definitely wrong. ☐

If they do not find iridium, the prediction may still be correct. ☐

Total [2]

3 Scientists wanted to find out whether smoking increases the risk of developing an eye disease called AMD.
Most AMD sufferers are partially blind.

a The scientists recorded the following statements.

A The greater the number of years a person smokes, and the more they smoke each day, the greater their risk of developing AMD.	
B Eye doctors have noticed a build-up of waste substances near the retinas of smokers' eyes.	
C 12% of AMD sufferers smoked 20 cigarettes a day for more than 40 years.	
D Substances in cigarette smoke may cause damage to cells in the retina of the eye.	
E Eye doctors have observed that people with AMD have damaged retinas.	

Write the letter **D** next to the **three** statements that are data.

Write the letter **E** next to the **one** statement that is part of an explanation.

Write the letter **C** next to the **one** statement that is a conclusion drawn from data. [3]

b The scientists used their explanation to make this prediction:

> Passive smokers have a greater risk of developing AMD than people who are not exposed to cigarette smoke.

They collected the following data:

▶ Of 100 non-smokers with AMD, 72 were passive smokers.
▶ Of 100 non-smokers without AMD, 66 were passive smokers.

Put a tick in the **two** boxes next to the statements that are true.

The data increase confidence in the explanation. ☐

The data prove the explanation is correct. ☐

The data agree with the prediction. ☐

The data decrease confidence in the explanation. ☐ [2]

Total [5]

4 Nearly 2000 people who lived near Lake Nyos in Cameroon died in 1986.

a Scientists wanted to find out why the people died.
They collected this data:

A Carbon dioxide is soluble in water.

B If carbon dioxide takes the place of air, people die from lack of oxygen.

C There is a volcano below Lake Nyos.

D Carbon dioxide gas is denser than air.

E Sometimes there are small Earth movements near Lake Nyos.

F If you shake a saturated solution of a gas, some of the gas escapes from solution.

G Carbon dioxide has no smell.

H Magma contains dissolved carbon dioxide.

I Carbon dioxide gas is invisible.

The scientists used their data to develop an explanation.
The explanation is in six parts.

Next to each part of the explanation, write one or two letters to show which data each part of the explanation accounts for.

One has been done for you.

Do not write in the shaded boxes.

Part of explanation	Data that this part of the explanation accounts for	
1 Carbon dioxide gas bubbles into the bottom of Lake Nyos.	C	
2 Carbon dioxide dissolves to make a saturated solution.		
3 There was a small Earth movement. This released 80 million cubic metres of carbon dioxide gas from the lake.		
4 Carbon dioxide gas filled the valleys around the lake.		
5 No one detected the carbon dioxide gas, so no one ran away.		
6 1700 people died.		

[8]

b Scientists predict that Lake Nyos will release carbon dioxide again in future. They expect more people to die. They do not know when this will happen.

Suggest one reason why the scientists cannot know when Lake Nyos will next release a large amount of carbon dioxide.

_____

_____ [1]

Total [9]

5 Scientists have studied earthquakes in areas near big, heavy structures made by humans.
They created this explanation:

> Big and heavy structures cause changes in the forces in the ground. These changes may cause earthquakes.

a Study the data in the table.

A	In 1967 there was an earthquake near a huge dam in India. The dam had just been finished.
B	Since 2003, there have been two earthquakes near the world's tallest building, Taipei 101. Taipei 101 was finished in 2003. Before Taipei 101, there were very few earthquakes in the area.
C	In 1967 there was an earthquake under a US mountain. A company had just injected huge amounts of waste into the mountain.
D	The earthquakes under Taipei 101 happened 10 km underground. The building does not affect underground forces at this depth.
E	In 2001 there was an earthquake in the North Sea. Companies have taken many tonnes of oil and gas from the area.

i Give the letters of two pieces of data that the explanation accounts for.

_____ [2]

ii Give the letter of one piece of data that conflicts with the explanation.

_____ [1]

H

b Governments plan to store carbon dioxide in big underground holes. A scientist uses the explanation in the box to make this prediction:

> There will be more earthquakes near carbon dioxide storage holes than there were in these areas before the storage holes were made.

The scientist collects data from now until 2020. Imagine the data shows that there had been five earthquakes near carbon dioxide storage holes. Before the holes were made, no earthquakes had been recorded in these areas.

Put ticks in the boxes that are true.

The data would not prove the explanation is correct. ☐

The data would agree with the prediction. ☐

The data would increase confidence in the explanation. ☐

The data would decrease confidence in the explanation. ☐

[2]

Total [5]

Risk

Don't buy that drink – it contains E211, that's sodium benzoate. We don't want to risk the kids' asthma and eczema getting worse.

*But **nothing is risk free**. Many scientific advances introduce new risks. Even if the kids drink only water, there's a risk of harm. A poisonous chemical could contaminate it.*

True, but it's so unlikely. I read about a Food Standards Agency report. They found that E211 can make the symptoms of asthma and eczema worse in children who already have them. Our kids' eczema and asthma are bad enough already. Let's minimize the risk of them getting worse.

Why are you lying out there in the sun at midday? Where's your sunscreen? It's dangerous to sunbathe – ultraviolet radiation from the sun hugely increases your risk of getting skin cancer. Each year, nearly 6000 British people get melanoma skin cancer.

*Yes, but there are **benefits** too. Sunlight helps you make vitamin D. You need this to strengthen your bones and muscles, and to boost your immune system. Anyway, I feel more confident when I've got a tan. And it's lovely and warm out here...*

*OK. I guess it's up to you. But I wish you wouldn't take the **risk**!*

H

1

The government is planning to build new nuclear power stations. A spokesperson says that they will safeguard future electricity supplies without contributing to global warming.

2

Well, they'd better not build one near here. I'm moving if they do.

What's your problem? The **chance** of a nuclear power station exploding is tiny.

3

But you've got to think of the **consequences** if it did explode. Two and a half thousand people died after the 1986 accident at Chernobyl.

And don't forget the risk of radioactive materials leaking out.

4

You're getting confused here. The actual measured risk of a leak is very low. I reckon you **think the risk is much higher than it really is** because ionizing radiation – and its effects – are **invisible**.

5

We've not even mentioned nuclear waste! We can't possibly know about the effects of this over the next thousand years.

Exactly. The government must not build them. It's simple – we just apply the **precautionary principle!** Better safe than sorry.

6

Have you forgotten the **ALARA principle**? The government needs to decide what level of risk is acceptable. Then it has to spend enough money to reduce the risk to this level. That's it – the risk will be As Low As is Reasonably Achievable!

Risk

1 Use the clues to fill in the grid.

1 Everything we do carries a risk of accident or h . . .

2 We can assess the size of a risk by measuring the c . . . of it happening in a large sample over a certain time.

3 Mobile phones are an example of a technological a . . . that brings with it new risks.

4 Radioactive materials emit i . . . radiation all the time.

5 The chance of a nuclear power station exploding is small. The c . . . of this happening would be devastating.

6 To apply the . . . principle, people must decide what level of risk is acceptable.

7 Some people think that the effects of a nuclear power station explosion are so terrible that the government should adopt the . . . principle and not build them at all.

8 Sometimes people think the size of a risk is bigger than it really is. Their perception of the size of the risk is greater than the . . . risk.

9 Nuclear power stations emit less carbon dioxide than coal-fired power stations. Some people think that this b . . . is worth the risk of building nuclear power stations.

10 Many people think that the size of the risk of flying in an aeroplane is greater than it really is. They p . . . that flying is risky because they don't fly very often.

11 It is impossible to reduce risk to zero. So people must decide what level or risk is a . . .

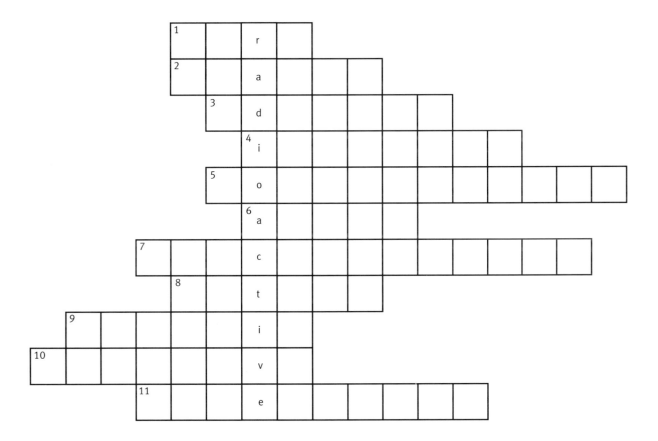

2 Draw a line to link two words on the circle.
Write a sentence on the line saying how the two words
are connected.
Repeat for as many pairs as you can.

risk

safe

benefits

chance

consequences

balance

unfamiliar

scientific advances

precautionary principle

actual risk

perceived risk

ALARA principle

Risk

1 Research shows that using sunbeds increases the risk of developing skin cancer. Ultraviolet radiation from sunbeds can cause eye cancer.

Some people who use sunbeds suffer from dry, bumpy, or itchy skin.

Many young people use sunbeds in tanning shops regularly.

a One tanning shop displays this notice.

Using our sunbeds	
▶ Lock the door.	☐
▶ Wear goggles.	☐
▶ Use the sunbed for a maximum of 15 minutes.	☐
▶ Wipe the sunbed clean after use.	☐
▶ Return your towel to reception.	☐
▶ Do not use the sunbed if you have lots of moles or freckles.	☐

Some of the information describes ways of reducing the risks of using sunbeds.

Write **R** in **three** boxes next to sentences that describe ways of reducing the risks. [3]

b i Suggest two reasons why many young people are willing to accept the risks of using sunbeds.

Reason 1 _____

_____

Reason 2 _____

_____ [2]

H

ii Three people made these comments about the risks of using sunbeds.

A I reckon the risk of getting skin cancer from sunbeds is tiny. My mum uses them all the time. She wouldn't if they were dangerous!

B I read an article in a medical journal. It says that the risk of developing skin cancer increases by 20% for every ten years you use sunbeds.

C Sunbeds are really dangerous. Your skin can go red and itchy when you use them. You can get eye cancer from them really quickly, too.

Give the letter of **one** comment that identifies an

actual risk of using sunbeds. _____

Give the letter of **one** comment that identifies a

perceived risk of using sunbeds. _____   [2]

c A Member of Parliament (MP) wants to ban under-18s from using sunbeds.

He does not want to stop adults from using them.

Use ideas about risk, benefit, and balance to discuss possible reasons for the MP wanting to ban under-18s, but not adults, from using sunbeds.

One mark is for a clear and ordered answer.

_____

_____

_____

_____

_____

_____   [3 + 1]

Total [11]

2 The Food Standards Agency (FSA) has found out that *Campylobacter* is the most common cause of food poisoning in Britain. Sufferers have severe diarrhoea and abdominal cramps.

The FSA did some research about *Campylobacter* in chickens. They bought chickens from shops. They found *Campylobacter* bacteria in 56% of the fresh chickens and 31% of the frozen chickens.

a The table lists ways of reducing the risk of becoming infected with *Campylobacter*.

Write the letter **I** next to actions that individual people can take.

Write the letter **G** next to actions that Governments can take.

A Cook chicken thoroughly.	
B Do not eat chicken.	
C Put advertisements on the radio to persuade people to cook chicken thoroughly.	
D Tell chicken farmers to apply very strict hygiene measures on their farms.	
E Wash your hands thoroughly after handling raw chicken.	
F Buy frozen chicken instead of fresh chicken.	

[2]

b Suggest two reasons why many people eat chicken, even when they know that this increases their risk of becoming infected with *Campylobacter*.

_____

_____

[2]

H

c The quotes show how four people react to the risk of becoming infected with *Campylobacter*.

Angus

I have heard that there is a risk of becoming infected with Campylobacter from eating chicken. So I will always make sure that the chicken I eat is properly cooked.

Brendan

I read in the newspaper that some Campylobacter can lead to severe long-term illness in a few people. I don't want to increase my risk of becoming very ill. So I will never eat chicken again.

Callum

I know that eating chicken carries a risk of becoming infected with Campylobacter. So I will take sensible precautions when I handle raw chicken.

Douglas

Only 1% of British people are infected with Campylobacter each year. So I don't believe the risk is worth worrying about.

The quotes show that one person is applying the precautionary principle.
Give his name.

_____

[1]

d A government has decided to apply the ALARA principle to the risk of becoming infected with *Campylobacter*. Write a sentence that the public can understand to state the government's policy on infection by *Campylobacter*.

_____

_____

_____

[2]

Total [5]

3 Read the article.

> ### Food for the brain
>
> A scientific report links poor diet to problems of behaviour and mood. The report says that people who do not eat enough vitamins, minerals, and essential fats are at increased risk of attention deficit disorder, depression, and schizophrenia.
>
> The report advises eating plenty of fruit, vegetables, fish, and seeds to prevent mental health problems. It also suggests not eating 'junk food', like burgers and chips.
>
> The scientists want the government to make sure that school meals include 'brain healthy' food to help prevent young people getting mental health problems.

    a **i** Draw a ring round the paragraph that identifies some risks of a poor diet.

        ii Draw a box around the paragraph that suggests ways of reducing the risks of getting mental health problems.   [2]

    b The article asks the government to take action.

        Use ideas about risk, costs, and benefits to write a paragraph arguing **for** *or* **against** this action.

        One mark is for quality of written communication.

_____

_____

_____

_____

_____

_____

[3 + 1]

Total [6]

4 Human activities cause an increase in greenhouse gases, such as carbon dioxide. Increasing amounts of greenhouse gases lead to global warming. Global warming causes rising sea levels and flooding.

The graphs show how greenhouse gas emissions from the USA and the European Union changed between 1990 and 2000.

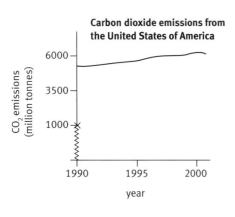

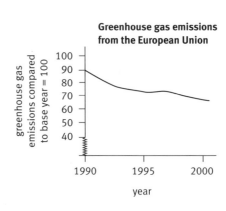

a Describe the trend for the European Union.

_____

_____ [1]

H

b Complete the sentences.

Use words from this list.

| benefits | chances | consequences | precautions |

If all countries have a similar trend to the USA, the _____

that the Earth's temperature will continue to increase are high. The

_____ of this for people who live on low-lying islands

could be devastating. [2]

c Some low-lying islands might disappear completely because of flooding caused by global warming. Are people who live on these islands more likely to want everyone in the world to adopt the **ALARA principle** or the **precautionary principle** towards reducing the risk of global warming? Give a reason for your choice.

_____

_____

_____

_____ [2]

Total [5]

Case study

The case study is your chance to find out more about a science-related issue that interests **you**. It's worth 20% of your total mark.

Choosing a topic

You need to find a science topic that is controversial – one that people have different opinions about. To get ideas, look in newspapers and magazines, or pick things up from television, radio, or the Internet.

It's best to choose from one of the topic types in the table.

Topic type	Examples	What to focus on
evaluating a claim where scientific knowledge is uncertain	▶ Is there life elsewhere in the Universe? ▶ Does using mobile phones increase risk of brain damage?	▶ relationships between data and explanations ▶ the quality of research behind different scientists' claims
helping to make a decision on a science-related issue	▶ Should a shopping street be pedestrianized to reduce air pollution? ▶ Should pre-implantation genetic screening be available free to anyone who wants to have a baby? ▶ Should Britain build new nuclear power stations?	▶ personal choice and values ▶ balancing risks and benefits of possible action
personal or social choices	▶ Should my child receive the MMR vaccine? ▶ Should I recycle all the plastic I use?	▶ personal and ethical issues ▶ using science to evaluate these issues

For the title, make up a question that you can answer by balancing evidence and opinions.

Selecting and using information (4 marks)

▶ Choose sources of information that are
   – varied, for example books, leaflets, newspaper articles, and websites
   – reliable: research reports from a university website may be more reliable than an individual's blog; journalists have their own opinions and don't always give balanced views; an organization that pays for a piece of science research may influence the research findings
   – relevant: if something is not relevant, throw it out!
▶ At the end of your report, include references to every source. Make it easy for someone else to find the information you have used (and check up on you!).
▶ Throughout your report, give the exact source of every quotation and opinion.

The science of the case (8 marks)

- Check what scientific knowledge you need in order to understand the issues in your study. You should be able to find most of it either in your textbook or in another source written at a similar level.
- Consider how well (or badly!) each opinion that you describe is supported by a science explanation.
- Look carefully at the quality of scientific evidence in each source to judge whether its claims are reliable.

In your report, you need to show that you've done all this – doing it but not writing about it counts for nothing! So include plenty of detail, and make sure that you link every claim or opinion to relevant scientific evidence.

If the science is too difficult, it is best to choose another topic.

Your conclusions (8 marks)

This is another chance to show how well you've understood ideas about science, particularly: data and their limitations; risk; making decisions.

In your conclusion

- Compare opposing evidence and views.
  - Report and evaluate arguments 'for' and 'against'
  - Compare these arguments carefully and critically
- Give conclusions and recommendations.
  - Suggest two or three different conclusions to show you realize that evidence can be interpreted in different ways.

Presenting your report (4 marks)

First of all, decide on an 'audience' for your report – this could be Year 9 students, a Member of Parliament, or any other individual or group.

Depending on the resources available, you might produce a formal written report, a newspaper article, a poster, or a PowerPoint presentation. Think about what is most appropriate for your audience and what you want to tell them. Whatever method you use, make sure that it looks attractive!

Then work on the following:

- The structure and organization of your report:
  - Put everything in a logical order, with plenty of subheadings.
  - Include page numbers and a contents list.
- Visual communication:
  - Include pictures, diagrams, charts, or tables to help your audience understand ideas and information.
- Spelling, punctuation and grammar:
  - Be concise – don't waste words!
  - Use relevant scientific words.
  - Check your spelling, punctuation, and grammar very carefully.

Data analysis

This is your chance to have a go at interpreting and analysing real data. It's worth 13.3% of your total mark.

Getting started

Start by doing a practical activity to collect the data you need. You can do this on your own or in a small group. Once you've collected some data yourself, you may be able to get the rest from other students, a teacher demonstration, or other sources.

Interpreting data

Follow the advice below, and you should get a high mark!

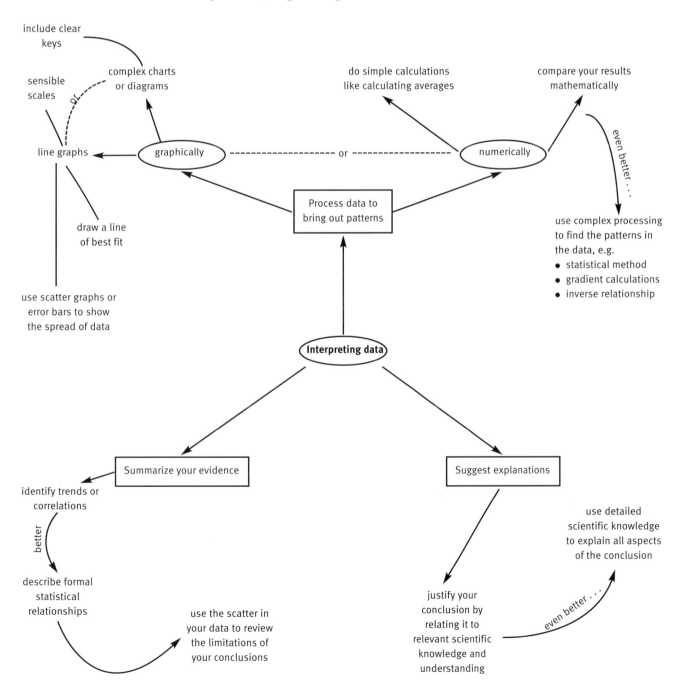

Evaluating data
Follow the advice below to achieve the very best you can!

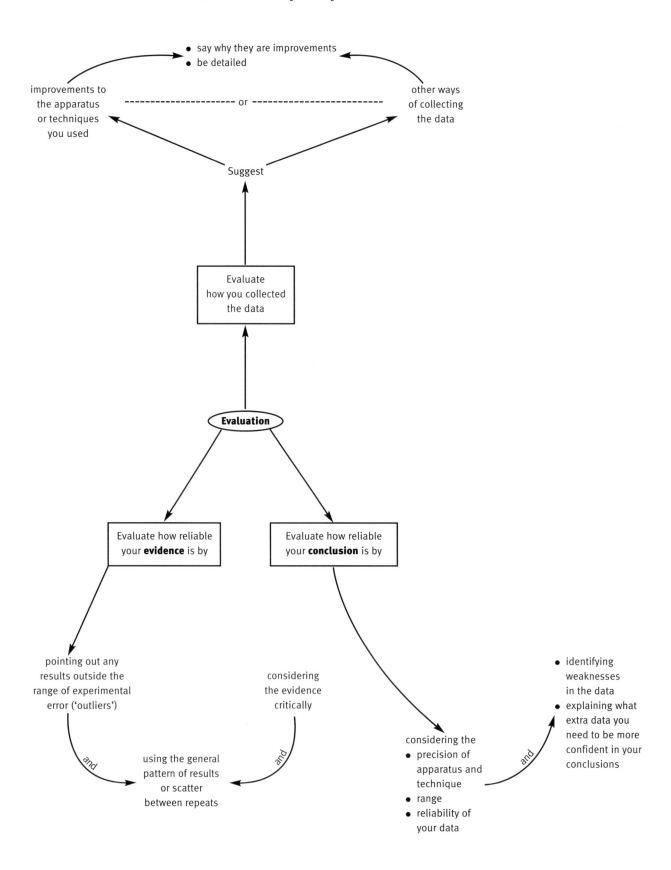

- say why they are improvements
- be detailed

improvements to the apparatus or techniques you used

------------------ or ------------------

other ways of collecting the data

Suggest

Evaluate how you collected the data

Evaluation

Evaluate how reliable your **evidence** is by

Evaluate how reliable your **conclusion** is by

pointing out any results outside the range of experimental error ('outliers')

and

using the general pattern of results or scatter between repeats

considering the evidence critically

and

considering the
- precision of apparatus and technique
- range
- reliability of your data

and

- identifying weaknesses in the data
- explaining what extra data you need to be more confident in your conclusions

Investigation

Your practical investigation counts for 33.3 % of your total grade. You will do the work in class. If you do more than one investigation, your teacher will choose the best one for your marks.

What you will do

In your investigation you will:

▶ choose a question to investigate
▶ select equipment and use it safely and appropriately
▶ make accurate and reliable observations

How your teacher will award marks

Your teacher will award marks under five headings.

Strategy

▶ Choose the task for your investigation.
▶ Decide how much data to collect.
▶ Choose equipment and techniques to give you precise and reliable data.

To get high marks here, choose a task which is not too simple. Plan to collect an appropriate range of precise and reliable data. Give reasons for your choice of equipment and techniques. Try to work as independently as possible.

Collecting data

▶ Work safely.
▶ Take careful and accurate measurements.
▶ Collect enough data and repeat it to check its reliability.
▶ Collect data across an appropriate range.
▶ Control other things that might affect your results.

To get high marks here, do preliminary work to decide the range. Collect data across the whole range. Repeat readings to make them as reliable as possible. Make sensible decisions about how to treat anomalous results (outliers). Use the apparatus skilfully to make precise readings. Try changing your techniques if you think that might give you better data.

Interpreting data

▶ Use charts, tables, diagrams, or graphs to show patterns in your results.
▶ Say what conclusions you can make from your data.
▶ Explain your conclusions using your science knowledge and understanding.

To get high marks here, label graph axes and table headings correctly. If appropriate, analyse your results mathematically. Summarize your evidence by identifying trends and correlations. Say whether there are any limitations in your data. Finally, use detailed scientific knowledge to explain your conclusion.

Evaluation

▶ Look back at your experiment and say how you could improve the method.
▶ Say how reliable you think your evidence is.
▶ Suggest improvements or extra data you could collect to be more confident in your conclusions.

To get high marks here, describe improvements to the method in detail. Say why they would be improvements. Use the pattern of your results, and the scatter between repeats, to help you to assess accuracy and reliability. Give reasons for any anomalous results. Say how confident you are in your conclusions, and give reasons for your decision. Describe in detail what extra data you would like to collect to make your conclusions more secure.

Presentation

▶ Write a full report of your investigation.
▶ Choose a sensible order for the different parts of your report, and lay it out clearly.
▶ Describe the apparatus you used and what you did with it.
▶ Show units correctly.
▶ Make sure your spelling, punctuation and grammar are accurate.
▶ Use scientific words when appropriate.

To get high marks here, state your investigation question clearly. Describe accurately and in detail how you did the practical work. Include all the data you collected, including repeat values. Make sure you record the data with appropriate accuracy and that you include all units. Record all your observations thoroughly and in detail.

Secondary data

As well as the data you collect, you may also use information from other people's work. This is secondary data. You can get secondary data from other students, the Internet, libraries, and textbooks. Or you might like to speak to a scientist or write to an organization. Think carefully about what you want to find out before looking for secondary data. This will help you to get the information you need without wasting time!

Answers

P1 Workout

1   **a** C   **b** A   **c** D   **d** A

2   **a** 3 hundred thousand
   b 4 thousand million
   c 10
   d 12 700
   e 1.4 million
   f 1000

3   Words/phrases **not** to cross out are: away from us; increases; Hubble's; expanding; thousand

4   From top to bottom: C, A, B

P1 GCSE-style questions

1   **a** Universe, Sun, Earth
   b Moon – a natural satellite; comet – a lump of rock held together by ice; asteroid – a body that looks like a small, rocky planet; star – a ball of hot gases
   c There was less light pollution 2000 years ago.
   d   **i** It orbits the Sun **or** it is big enough to be spherical.
      ii Its orbit overlaps Neptune's, so it has another object in its orbit.

2   **a** From centre: core, mantle, crust
   b 1C; 2D; 3B; 4A

3   **a** Milky Way
   b Thousands of millions
   c The stars of Andromeda emit light.
   d   **i** They are at different stages of their life cycles.
      ii Everything we know about stars and galaxies comes only from the radiation they emit; Scientists use a star's relative brightness to measure its distance from Earth. But relative brightness also depends on what stage in its life cycle a star is at.
      iii The distance light travels in one year

4   **a** 10 cm/year
   b B because C and A **or** B because A and C
   c 1B; 2C; 3A

P2 Workout

1   Microwaves, light, X-rays

2   Ionizing radiations: ultraviolet, X-rays, gamma rays Radiations that cause a heating effect only: light, infrared, microwaves

3   The satellite both absorbs and transmits radiation. The air transmits radiation. The transmitter is a source of radiation. The TV is a detector. It absorbs radiation. The energy deposited here by a beam of radiation depends on the number of photons and the energy of one photon. The hill reflects radiation. The energy that arrives at a surface each second is the intensity of the radiation.

5   Ionizing; chemical reactions; vibrate; intensity; time

6   Carbon dioxide only: A, G, H, I
Ozone only: B, C, E, J
Both: D, F (accept I)

P2 GCSE-style questions

1   **a** Infrared – transmitting messages between remote controls and televisions; microwaves – transmitting messages between phone masts; radio waves – broadcasting television programmes
   b Source emits radiation; glass transmits radiation; metal reflects radiation; water in food absorbs radiation.
   c Metal walls prevent microwave radiation leaving the oven **or** cannot operate oven when door is open.

2   **a** Ultraviolet radiation is a type of ionizing radiation; ultraviolet radiation can make cells grow in an uncontrolled way; ultraviolet radiation makes molecules more likely to react chemically; ultraviolet radiation damages the DNA of cells.
   b Clothes **or** sunscreen
   c   **i** Ozone molecules absorb ultraviolet radiation.
      ii Ozone protects living things from the Sun's UV radiation. Anything that destroys ozone – such as some chemicals in aerosols – therefore increases the risk of humans getting skin cancer and eye cataracts.

3   **a** The intensity of the radiation arriving at Helen's phone is less **or** the distance between Helen and the source is greater.
   b   **i** Decreases
      ii Radiation spreads over a larger and larger surface area.
   c Vibrate; intensity; time

4   **a**   **i** Combustion, respiration
      ii Photosynthesis, dissolving in water
   b   **i** The rate at which carbon dioxide was added to the atmosphere was the same as the rate at which it was removed from the atmosphere.
      ii Humans have burned more fossil fuels; humans have cut down forests and burned the wood.
   c   **i** Rising sea levels; changing climates
      ii Methane, water vapour

P3 Workout

1   Left-hand person: A, C, D, E; right-hand person: B, C, D, E, F

2   Ionizing; ground; space; atoms; medical treatment; ionizing; chemically; kill; damage

3   1B **or** C; 2A; 3D; 4F; 5C **or** B; 6E

5   **a** 65 units
   b 35%

6   **a** T   **b** F   **c** T   **d** T   **e** T
   f F   **g** F   **h** T   **i** F

7   **a** A and B; D and E
   b F
   c E
   d B and C

P3 GCSE-style questions

1   **a**   **i** Radioactive
      ii Gamma radiation can penetrate deep inside Arthur's body to reach his tumour.
   b   **i** Kill them
      ii The gamma radiation also kills healthy cells.
   c   **i** To prevent ionizing radiation leaving the room
      ii To minimize the dose of ionizing radiation s/he receives

2 a The activity of the Cs-137 source decreases over time; the half-life of Cs-137 is 30 years.
b 2.5 g
c Unstable; stable

3 a D A C G B
b Rate, boron, neutrons
c Low level – pack it in drums; medium level – mix it with concrete; high level – very difficult to store safely

P4 Workout

1 a B **b** A **c** B **d** A

2 Rope 10 N to right; tricycle 120 N to right; trolley no resultant force

3 Picture 1 – C; picture 2 – B; picture 3 – A

4 a F **b** T **c** F **d** F **e** T
f F **g** T

5 A B D E C

6 a T **b** T **c** T **d** F **e** T
f T **g** F

7 a 200 m/min **b** 40 m/s
c 18 m/s **d** 4 cm/s

8 In order along the curve: B, A, C, E, D, F

9 a 0 km/h **b** 7.5 km/h

10 a 88 000 kg m/s **b** 304 kg m/s **c** 13.5 kg m/s

11 In order along the curve: A, B, D, F, E, C

12 15 000 Ns

13 a 30 000 J **b** 1 250 000 J **c** 58 J

14 a 3 J **b** 3 J **c** 7.8 m/s

15 1 interaction, 2 kinetic, 3 tachographs, 4 resultant, 5 friction, 6 average, 7 reaction, 8 potential, 9 driving, 10 momentum, 11 negative

P4 GCSE-style questions

1 a i D to E
ii Stationary from B to C; moving at a steady speed from C to D – this is the fastest part of the fire engine's journey
iii 1 km/min
b 12 m/s
c

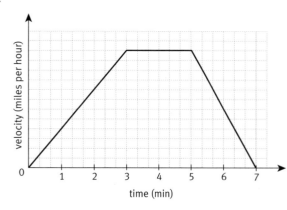

2 a Bottom row is correct
b Increases
c The counter–force and driving force are equal and opposite.

3 a i All statements are true except the first one
ii 1500 J
iii 1500 J
b 300 J

4 a 16 200 kg m/s
b 1 620 000 N
c Seatbelts stretch during a collision; seatbelts reduce the force that the driver experiences; seatbelts make you move forward more slowly during a collision.

5 a 45 000 J
b 45 000 J

P5 Workout

1 Electrons, negatively, negative, positive, attractive, repel

2 All conductors–contain charges that are free to move; insulators–do not conduct electricity; insulators–include polythene, wood, and rubber; insulators–do not contain charges that are free to move; metal conductors–contain charges that are free to move; metal conductors–contain electrons that are free to move; in a complete circuit charges are not used up; in a complete circuit–the battery makes free charges flow in a continuous loop.

3 Hotter, moving, stationary, more, smaller

4 Ammeter $\textcircled{A}$; voltmeter $\textcircled{V}$; cell $—|\!—$;

power supply $—|\!\vdash\!|—$ (battery) or $—\overset{+}{\circ}\ \bar{\circ}—$ (DC)

or $—\circ\!\sim\!\circ—$ (AC); lamp $\bigotimes$; switch $—\!\!\swarrow\!\circ—$;

LDR $—\boxed{\ }\!—$; fixed resistor $—\boxed{\ }—$;

variable resistor $—\boxed{\diagup}\!—$; thermistor $—\boxed{\diagup}—$

5 a B **b** A **c** B

6 Circuit 1: B F H; circuit 2: A C D; both circuits: E G

7 a 14.23 Ω **b** 30 Ω

8 a 0.4 A **b** 3 V

9 Clockwise from top: the same as, volts, voltage, push, potential energy, less

10 a Both are 100 mA
b i Resistor on right
ii Greatest; more work is done by charge flowing through a large resistance than through a small one.
c i 0.6 V
ii the p.d.s across the components add up to the p.d. across the battery

11 Computer – energy transferred is 0.5 kWh
Kettle – energy transferred is 0.09 kWh
Toaster – power rating is 1 200 W or 1.2 kW
Mobile phone charger – power rating is 0.02 kW

12 a £ 0.24 **b** £ 0.10

13 Coil, current, out, pole

14 a 3.91 A **b** 0.870 A

15 11.5 V

16 1 resistance, 2 current, 3 kWh, 4 power, 5 V, 6 parallel, 7 voltmeter, 8 Ω, 9 generator, 10 induction, 11 R, 12 direct, 13 AC, 14 A, 15 efficiency, 16 DC

P5 GCSE-style questions

1 a When the switch is closed, the battery makes free charges in the circuit move; the metal wires contain electrons that are free to move; when the switch is closed there is a flow of charge.

b Voltage, current, resistance, current, current, resistance

2 a i Voltmeter connected in parallel to the heater
ii 1.2 Ω

b Moving electrons bump into stationary atoms in the wire.

3 a 788 kWh
b : 24
c 245 hours

4 a i 230 V **ii** 230 V
b 3 amps
c Stays the same
d i 14.4 amps
ii Fridge – current is smallest through this appliance whilst the voltage across all the appliances is the same.

5 a Increase the number of coils, increase the strength of the magnet, put an iron core inside the coil.
b i Iron, induces
ii 120

P6 Workout

1 Vibrations are at right angles – transverse – x-rays, water waves and waves on a rope; vibrations are in the same direction – longitudinal – sound waves. Other answers possible.

2 Wave – a disturbance moving through a material medium – the material a wave travels through; frequency – the number of waves a source makes every second; source – this vibrates to make a wave.

3 See diagram on page 155.

4 a 333 m/s **b** 0.333 km/s

5 A – refraction; B – diffraction; C – reflection

6 a 2 m/s **b** 340 m/s

7 Reinforce, constructive, B, cancel out, destructive, A

8 a 1500 m **b** 0.6 m

9 Frequency, speed, wavelength, refraction, faster, towards

10 a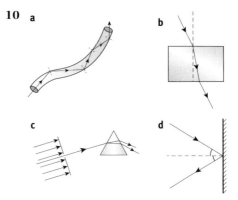

11 Digital signals transmit information with higher quality than analogue signals. This is because noise can be removed from digital signals but not from analogue signals.

12 1 radio, 2 infrared, 3 frequency, 4 variation, 5 receiver, 6 AM, 7 analogue, 8 digital, 9 interference, 10 decode, 11 – noise

P6 GCSE-style questions

1 a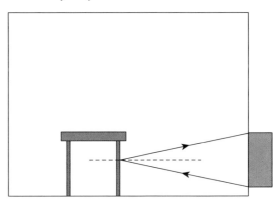

b C

c 10 000 000 000

d Microwaves are reflected by metal

2 a Amplitude = 30 m; frequency = 2 waves per hour; wavelength = 3 km

b i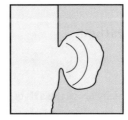

ii Diffraction
c i Refraction
ii Arrow at right angles to crests of waves in shallow water

3 a Top – AM; middle – digital; bottom – FM
b B E D C A
c With digital signals, 0 and 1 can still be recognized even if noise has been picked up. So the signal can be 'cleaned up' by removing the noise. Noise cannot be removed from analogue signals.

4 a Transmitted

b Absorbs – If the intensity of the light that comes out of the brain is less than expected, the brain might be bleeding. This suggests that blood absorbs light, so the intensity of transmitted light decreases.

c In one second, a different number of photons arrives at each detector.

d i One of: X-rays damage living cells and can cause cancer; X-rays will be absorbed by the bone of the skull, so will give no useful information.

ii Microwaves have a heating effect, so will heat up brain tissue causing great damage.

P7A   Workout

1 Time for the Earth to rotate once about its axis – 23 hours 56 minutes; time for the Earth to complete one orbit of the Sun – 365¼ days; a solar day – 24 hours; time for the Moon to move across the sky once – 25 hours; time for the Moon to orbit the Earth – about 28 days; difference between a solar day and a sidereal day – 4 minutes.

2 full moon = light circle = position 5
new moon = dark circle = position 1
first quarter = circle with left-hand half shaded = position 3
last quarter = circle with right-hand half shaded = position 7

3 Sun, Solar, Planets, sidereal, axis, solar, orbit, 4 minutes

4 a F   **b** F   **c** T   **d** T   **e** F
f F   **g** T   **h** T   **i** F   **j** T

5 moon, planet, star, solar system, galaxy, universe

6 a See diagram on page 94.
b 3–5
c X marked on circle between Sun and Earth.
Y marked on circle at opposite side of Earth from Sun.
d The Moon's orbit is tilted by about 5° relative to the plane of the Earth's orbit.

7 a Astronomer, red, orbit, astrolabe, moon, navigation, umbra, phase, sidereal, constellation
b Retrograde. The apparent backward motion of a planet relative to the fixed stars, caused by the relative positions of the Earth and planet.

P7A   GCSE-style questions

1 a constellation
b two
c The Earth has rotated
d It is the Pole Star, directly above the axis of rotation/the North Pole.
e After six months, the Earth has moved halfway around its orbit. Orion is now in the direction of the Sun and can't be seen due to the sunlight (see diagram on page 93).
f The Moon orbits the Earth (see diagram on page 94).
g You should have drawn a full circle.
h Circle drawn with crescent shaded on right-hand side. Part of the Moon is in shadow, since its position has changed relative to the Sun and Earth.

2 a The shadow of the Moon falling on the Earth/the Moon coming between the Sun and the Earth

b The Moon's orbit is tilted relative to the Earth's orbit about the Sun, so that only rarely are Sun, Moon and Earth in alignment.
c 5°
d New moon
e The shadow of the Earth falling on the Moon/the Earth coming between the Sun and the Moon

3 a Observe the position of the object
Over several nights
If its position changes relative to the fixed stars then it is a planet.
One mark for clarity of answer.
b A star is a source of light and heat/is luminous.
A planet orbits a star/is seen by reflected light.
Both star and planet must be mentioned to get the mark.

4 a i 24 hours
ii 23 hours 56 minutes
iii 24 hours 49 minutes
iv 23 hours 56 minutes
b i The apparent movement of the Sun or Moon or stars across the sky
ii The retrograde/complicated movement of the planets across the sky

P7B   Workout

1 Magnification – how much bigger (in angle) the image is than the object; resolving power – how well an instrument distinguishes objects that are close together; dioptres – the unit for measuring the power of a lens; convex lens – a lens that is thicker in the centre than the edges, causing light rays to converge; concave lens – a lens that is thicker at the edges than in the centre, causing light rays to diverge; refraction – the change in direction of a ray of light as it passes from one material into another; reflection – the bouncing back of light at the boundary between two materials; diffraction – the spreading out of a wave as it passes through a small aperture; focal length – the distance between the focus and the centre of a lens.

2 ☐ ✓ ☐ ✓
☐ ✓ ☐ ✓

3 3 1 2

4 a Diagram showing image marked 6 cm from lens, 3 cm below principal axis.
b real, inverted, magnified

5 a 2, 5, 10, 2.5 (hint: don't forget to change cm to metres)
b Nikhita's
c Nikhita's and Guy's
d Nikhita's
e 60 cm
f 5 times

6 a bigger, wavelength
b diffraction, resolving power, aperture, wavelength
c concave, reflecting, lenses, easier

7 a T   **b** F   **c** F   **d** T
e T   **f** F   **g** T

8 Disadvantages of space telescopes are that they are – expensive to set up and maintain; computers are used to control telescopes because they can – enable a telescope to track a distant star while the earth rotates, allow the telescope to be used by an astronomer not at the observatory; international cooperation in astronomy allows – the cost of new major telescopes to be shared, the pooling of scientific expertise; in deciding where to site a new observatory it is necessary to consider – the amount of light pollution, common local weather conditions, the environmental and social impact of the project.

9 aperture, lens, Chile, objective, atmosphere, concave, orbit, eyepiece, Jodrell. Telescope

P7B GCSE-style questions

1 a Reflector because it has a mirror
b Sharing costs, sharing expertise
c It is above the atmosphere.
It avoids absorption and refraction effects of the atmosphere.
d Advantage: can detect frequencies of radiation that can't be detected on Earth due to absorption by the atmosphere. Disadvantages: cost/difficult to maintain.

2 a Any one from:
Image can be processed directly, e.g. improve contrast, reduce noise, add false colour.
Images can be sent directly to astronomers in other places.
It is not necessary for the astronomer to be at the telescope.
Faster.
More images can be taken with the telescope during a single session.
Don't need to develop the film.
Saves the cost of the film.
Or any other relevant suggestion.
b Any one from:
To enable telescopes to move, tracking stars as the earth rotates.
To share information with other scientists.
To control telescopes remotely.
To locate particular areas of the sky quickly.
Or any other relevant suggestion.
1 mark for answer and 1 for explanation.

3 a See diagram on page 106.
b Rays from the top of the object go to the bottom of the image.

4 a A marked as objective lens.
Horizontal line marked as principal axis.
Distance from centre of lens to place where rays cross marked as focal length of A.
b The stars are a very long way away so the angle they make at the telescope is too small to be measured.
c

✓	✓
✓	✓

d 1/0.80 = 1.25 dioptres
e 80 + 5 = 85 cm

f The increase in the angle made by the image at the eye compared with the angle made by the object
g 80/5 = 16
h Increase the diameter of lens A

P7C Workout

1 electrons, charged, energy, ionisation, nucleus, protons, neutrons, fusion, small, join, energy, temperature, pressure, core

2 Labels as page 118 of workbook.

3 Most alpha particles pass through gold foil undeflected – an atom is mostly empty space; the gas in a street lamp only emits light of a few frequencies (line spectra) – electrons can only possess certain energy values; a few alpha particles were deflected through large angles by the gold foil – atoms have a very small, dense, positive nucleus; gases can be compressed easily – there are large empty spaces between the particles.

4 □ □ ✓ □

5 □ ✓ ✓ □

6 a C   **b** A   **c** D   **d** D   **e** A

7 A E F D C B

8 Gravity pulls gases together to form a protostar
Main sequence star fusing hydrogen into helium
Red giant fusing helium into larger nuclei
White dwarf gradually cools
Red supergiant fusing helium and other nuclei to make much larger nuclei up to iron
Supernova
Neutron star
Black hole

9 Largest curve is hottest and white.
Middle curve is yellow.
Lowest curve is coolest and red.

10 a protons   **b** absolute zero   **c** gravity
d protostar   **e** strong   **f** hole   **g** fusion
h core   **i** supernova   **j** photosphere   **k** gold
l electron   **m** kelvin   **n** nucleus   **o** convective zone
p giant   **q** supergiant   **r** star
s pressure   **t** energy   **u** atom   **v** light
w dwarf   **x** particles

P7C GCSE-style questions

1 a Its temperature
b Total amount of radiation given out by star
c 'Hottest' written on uppermost curve
d Absorption by the atmosphere
e The chemical elements present in the star
f Electron movement within atoms

2 a Gas particles are moving in random directions.
Particles colliding with the sides of the container create a force on the sides.
b Particles move faster.

Answers

c Pressure increases as the particles hit the sides of the box more often and harder.

3 a A few alpha particles deflected backwards through large angles
b Most alpha particles not deflected
c Protons and neutrons
d Strong nuclear force

4 a From the peak frequency of its spectrum
b The position of the black lines in its spectrum
c Gravity pulls the hydrogen gas together.
The temperature and pressure of the hydrogen increases.
Eventually fusion will start in the core.
d (nuclear) fusion
e Hydrogen → Helium + Energy
f Helium is fusing to make heavier elements
g It has been made from the remains of an earlier star.
h White dwarf
i When helium fusion stops
j B because of its high mass
k Black hole, neutron star

5 a Photosphere
b By convection
c 5227 °C
d Temperature increases the speed of the nuclei so they have more energy when they collide. Pressure increases the number of collisions.
e Gravity
f i When the core hydrogen is depleted
ii Its mass
g −270 °C
h At zero Kelvin the particles would not be moving at all. It is not possible for them to go any slower than stopped!

P7D Workout

1 Parallax – how closer stars seem to move over time relative to more distant ones; parsec – the distance to a star with a parallax angle of one second of arc; light-year – the distance that light travels in one year; nebula – a fuzzy object seen in the night sky, either a distant galaxy or cloud of gas; galaxy – a group of millions of stars; Cepheid variable – a star whose brightness varies periodically.

2 a A **b** B **c** D **d** B

3 a parallax angle **b** Cepheid variable
c speed, distance **d** intrinsic brightness
e intrinsic brightness, distance away

4 ...within our galaxy.
...measure the distance to one nebula.
...it is much further away than any other stars in our galaxy. Curtis.

5 Graph labels: vertical – speed of recession, horizontal – distance of galaxy from Earth
period, variable, distance, light, away, Universe, red shift, galaxy, speed, graph, Hubble, uncertain, measure, accurately.

6 a 4.0, 3.5, 2.7
b the parallax angles are too small to be measured
c 4.3 light years **d** 6000 km/s

e 10^{21} km **f** 2.3×10^{-18} s^{-1}

7 a F **b** T **c** T **d** F **e** T
f T **g** T **h** T **i** F

8 A D C B

9 Milky Way, nebula, Shapley, Cepheid variable, lightyear, temperature, redshift. Leavitt. Discovering the correlation between the period and intrinsic brightness of Cepheid variable stars.

P7D GCSE-style questions

1 a Cepheid variable
b Answer in range 2–2.1 days
c Answer in range 2070–2200
d The distance to the star

2 a The apparent shift of an object against a more distant background as the position of the observer changes.
b Sirius A because its parallax angle is the greatest
c 1/0.286 = 3.5 parsecs
d The distance light travels in one year
e We see the light that left the star at an earlier time in history

3 a A collection of thousands of millions of stars held together by gravity
b Milky Way
c In another galaxy, because the distances between galaxies is measured in megaparsecs
d 2.3×10^{-18} s^{-1}
e It is hard to get an accurate measurement for the distance to very distant galaxies.

4 a The observer brightness depends on both the distance away and the intrinsic brightness. A star might be further away but have a greater intrinsic brightness due to its greater temperature or size.
b The distance to a star with a parallax angle of one second of arc
c Nebulae/nebulas
d Whether nebulae were objects within the Milky Way or separate galaxies outside it.

Index

Index